Sir Gawain and the Green Knight

Sir Gawain and the Green Knight

Translated, with notes, by
Joseph Glaser

Introduction by
Christine Chism

Hackett Publishing Company, Inc.
Indianapolis/Cambridge

15 14 13 12 11   1 2 3 4 5 6 7

For further information, please address
Hackett Publishing Company, Inc.
P.O. Box 44937
Indianapolis, Indiana 46244-0937

www.hackettpublishing.com

Cover design by Brian Rak
Interior design by Mary Vasquez
Composition by Agnew's, Inc.
Printed at Edwards Brothers, Inc.

Library of Congress Cataloging-in-Publication Data

Gawain and the Grene Knight. English & English (Middle English)

    Sir Gawain and the green knight / translated, with notes, by
Joseph Glaser ; introduction by Christine Chism.
        p. cm.
    ISBN 978-1-60384-619-6 (cloth) — ISBN 978-1-60384-618-9 (pbk.)
    1. Gawain (Legendary character)—Romances.   2. Knights and
knighthood—Poetry.   3. Arthurian romances.   I. Glaser, Joseph,
1942– II. Title.
PR2065.G3A336 2011
821.1—dc22

                                                            2011017922

The paper used in this publication meets the minimum requirements of American
National Standard for Information Sciences—Permanence of Paper for Printed
Library Materials, ANSI Z39.48–1984.

⊗

Contents

Acknowledgments

I want to thank two expert readers for their valuable (and sometimes face-saving) suggestions: Jordi Sánchez-Martí of the University of Alicante and Ad Putter of the University of Bristol. Professor Putter was particularly generous with his help, though he is in no way responsible, of course, for the use I made of it. Closer to home, my colleagues Jim Flynn and John Reiss read the text at various stages and never failed to offer improvements. Mary Vasquez, project editor at Hackett, was most resourceful and efficient, and senior editor Brian Rak was steadily encouraging and helpful, as always. All of them made this a better book than I could have managed on my own.

Introduction

Sir Gawain and the Green Knight is a mystery in both the Middle English and present-day English senses of the word. Middle English *mistere* denoted "artistry" or "craft" as one of its meanings, and *Sir Gawain and the Green Knight* is a wonderfully crafted work, a romancer's romance that delivers some of the most beautiful English poetry of any age. At the same time, it is a mystery in the modern sense because it is so open-ended. From its unforgettable opening scene, in which the Green Knight greets the knights of Camelot with a battle-axe in one hand and a festive branch of holly in the other, the poem delights in conundrums. Even at the end, as Gawain returns to Arthur's court a sadder but wiser man, the poem allows the reader at least three possible interpretations of his adventure. The poem's circular structure and two embedded plots give an impression of exquisite symmetry, but the symmetries themselves pose conundrums. The poem raises more questions than it answers.

Authorship

To deepen the poem's mystery, less is known about the *Gawain*-poet than about virtually any widely read late-medieval writer—less even than about his two main rivals, Geoffrey Chaucer and William Langland. Chaucer remains enigmatic as a practicing poet, but he left almost five hundred life records about his fourteenth-century career in royal service. Langland, generally acknowledged as the author of *Piers Plowman*, is known in part from internal evidence in his poem, whose narrator identifies himself by name. The *Gawain*-poet, in contrast, neither left records nor named himself but instead clung to the anonymity that was the norm among fourteenth-century writers of romance in England. He is known as either the *Gawain*-poet or the *Pearl*-poet, depending on which of his major works is under scrutiny.

All four of the poems attributed to him, *Gawain, Pearl, Cleanness,* and *Patience,* are widely associated with the same author because they share similar traits and survive in a single manuscript from around 1400—British Library, Cotton Nero A.x.—a manuscript notable for its full-sized illuminations. The *Gawain*-poet is thus a cipher whose historical identity remains elusive.

Although the *Gawain*-poet may never be firmly identified, we know several things about him. First, he used an east Cheshire dialect, which locates him in the northwest Midlands of England, close to the Chester/Staffordshire border and the border of Wales. Cheshire was one of the provinces most closely tied to the royal court and its politics. Richard II's reign (1377–1399) was particularly eventful for Cheshire: Richard invested Cheshire as a full principality, recruited many Cheshire nobles and gentry into his service, and built up what amounts to his own standing army of Cheshire archers. Cheshire had few great estates and large towns; its countryside was a mixture of smaller holdings and wild, undeveloped areas. Yet the late-medieval population of Chester, its regional center, was very diverse and included Welsh, Irish, Manx, and Continental merchants as well as travelers and traders from London, the south of England, and other parts of the realm. The *Gawain*-poet thus had the cultural resources of a lively and distinctive province in continual transaction with other parts of England, and he may well have been familiar with London, the royal court at Westminster, Wales, and places farther afield.

We do not know how the *Gawain*-poet made a living or from what class he came, but he probably received clerical training. In the fourteenth century, many clerics took minor orders and learned how to read Latin, participate in liturgical services, and interpret the Bible, the church fathers, and medieval commentaries. Some eventually took major orders and became priests but others did not, instead seeking lay employment in royal or noble service, as lawyers at the Inns of Court or as accountants among the gentry. The *Gawain*-poet's other poems, the homiletic poems *Pearl, Cleanness,* and *Patience,* expertly collate Vulgate and other Latin sources to retell the stories of Jonah, Noah's Flood, Nebuchadnezzar, Balthazar and the writing on the wall, and the destruction of Sodom and Gomorrah. Yet their narrator does not speak as a priest or imparter of authoritative lessons and sacraments. Rather, as Ad Putter has argued, he identifies himself with a lay audience receiving such lessons and sacraments and pondering their difficulties. *Patience* and *Cleanness* illustrate the conflicts implicit in human attempts to understand and accept divine truths that often seem terrible. *Pearl* presents a long dialogue between a grieving man and his dead, celestially transfigured child that is transacted across an impassible river; the poem dramatizes the difficulty of reconciling the narrator's vision of his redeemed daughter with the experience of mourning her. At the end, in a fit of frustration, the narrator leaps into the river and wakes himself, putting an end to the vision. In all this, the *Gawain*-poet displays a measure of biblical and doctrinal learning that seems to set him apart from the audience with which he identifies. But that learning is deployed for purposes that are, properly speaking, neither clerical nor laical but rather very much the poet's own; the homiletic poems dramatize the difficulties of biblical interpretation, showing an interest in interpretive impasses and paradoxes that will also permeate his sole poetic foray into courtly romance—*Sir Gawain and the Green Knight.*

Sir Gawain and the Green Knight fills in another detail about its poet: he was familiar with life in a noble household. The poem is saturated with representations of the habits, religious rituals, festivals, and hobbies of late-medieval English aristocratic life—complete with up-to-the-minute castle architecture, estate landscaping, hunting, clothing, heraldry, and fashions of polite conversation, "crowning examples of courtly discourse" (l. 917). We do not know what kind of noble household the *Gawain*-poet frequented, whether a manor, a noble household, or the royal court itself, but it is a safe guess that he was a household functionary who traveled between London and the provinces during the last half of the fourteenth century. The manuscript gives us some help with the poem's latest possible date, as the manuscript was written around 1400, but the poem has been linked to many fourteenth-century historical developments, from Edward III's establishment of the knightly Order of the Garter in the 1340s (whose motto a scribe has added to the end of the manuscript) to Richard's youthful court in the early 1380s and his deposition in 1399.

Because we do not know the social circles in which the *Gawain*-poet circulated, we cannot know what his original audience was like—

whether the poem was read aloud for Christmas entertainment at a small manorial estate in Cheshire, in the company of an itinerant noble household, for the amusement of Edward III's diverse court, or for Richard II's youthful and exclusive court. The poem's narrator, however, conjures up an imagined audience at once thoroughly conventional and suggestive. At the beginning, he invokes the kind of generic audience that would listen to a minstrel's lay for entertainment after a feast—a gathering, that is, of polite-minded gentlefolk capable of being captivated by the poet's skill and illustrious subject matter. And he proposes to regale it with a wondrous story concerning one of the greatest subject matters of all—that of King Arthur and Britain.

Bliss and Blunder: The Matter of Britain

The story of King Arthur and his knights was one of the great legendary story cycles of medieval Europe. Roughly referred to as the Matter of Britain, it stands alongside the Matter of France (stories of the eighth-century Emperor Charlemagne) and the Matter of Rome (stories about the Trojan War, the foundation of the Roman Empire, and the campaigns of Alexander the Great). For centuries, across England, France, Germany, and other European countries, writers of history and romance amplified the Arthurian legend, building on each other's texts and inventing their own incidents and adventures. King Arthur's historical origin is unclear, but early sources suggest that he may have been a Welsh war leader who defended Britain from the Saxon invaders at the beginning of the sixth century. Arthur's name is mentioned in early Welsh lore poetry, and one of the stories in the Welsh *Mabinogi,* the story of Culhwch and Olwen, written around 1100, features the hero Culhwch's visit to Arthur's court, where he requests help on a difficult quest from Arthur and his men.

Yet Arthur very early became a topic of interest to writers in non-Welsh languages. The Latin *Historia Brittonum* attributed to Nennius, a ninth-century Welsh monk, tells of Arthur and his twelve battles as it recounts other marvels of the British Isles and elaborates on the historical accomplishments of ancient British leaders. Nennius' version of ancient British history demonstrates pride in the

British landscape and British history, and his work was a great resource to later writers even more interested in establishing workable connections with Britain's deep past.

The first writer really to mine the political and narrative potential of ancient British history and the Welsh legend of Arthur was the twelfth-century cleric Geoffrey of Monmouth (c.1100–1155). Geoffrey lived, worked, and wrote in the long aftermath of the Norman Conquest of England (1066), an era of simultaneous Norman empire building and political unrest. Geoffrey hailed from the Welsh border country, was probably a member of the Norman gentry, was perhaps of Breton descent, and may have known some Welsh. He wrote three major works: the *Prophetiae Merlini* (*The Prophecies of Merlin*); the *Historia Regum Britanniae* (*The History of the Kings of Britain,* a chronicle of ancient British history); and the *Vita Merlini* (*The Life of Merlin*). Geoffrey was the writer who decisively shaped Arthur for later writers, and he reinvented Merlin as well by amalgamating two ancient Welsh Myrddins: one a prophet, the other a poet.

Geoffrey's *Historia* was innovative in a number of significant ways. Geoffrey departs from the dominant historiographical traditions of his day by concentrating not on the history of the church and its expansion but rather on secular history. His chronicle constructs a millennia-spanning genealogy of British kings, from Britain's legendary settlement to the seventh-century leader Cadwallader. He is thus filling in a part of British prehistory that no one else had written about; most medieval historians had followed the seventh-century cleric Bede and begun their history with the sixth-century Anglo-Saxon invasions. Geoffrey also draws fluidly on epic traditions deriving from Virgil's *Aeneid* to glorify the foundation of Britain by the refugee Brutus. Brutus was a descendant of Aeneas who, like his forebear, became the leader of a group of wandering Trojans. Yet unlike Virgil's backward-yearning Aeneas, Geoffrey's Brutus focuses singlemindedly on a future. Brutus is a parricide, inspired by a need for freedom and a vision of lasting sovereignty endowed by the Roman goddess Diana. As the founder of a race of warrior kings in the Britain that now bears his name, Brutus ousted a primeval population of giants and at his death left the realm to his sons as three realms: England, Scotland, and Wales. It is this foundational era that *Sir Gawain and the Green Knight* recalls in its opening lines, in which Britain springs from the ashes of Troy.

Yet, as *Sir Gawain* suggests, Geoffrey's early history of Britain was neither peaceful nor stable: "Brash lads have bred there, bold lovers of battle. / In days that dawned after, they dealt out great dole" (ll. 21–22). The first half of Geoffrey's *Historia* depicts a relentless alternation of civil turmoil and reconsolidation, with the accomplishments of one regime scattered in the next generation by fratricidal conflict between heirs. One of the stories Geoffrey relates is a case in point—the story of King Leir and his daughters, which Shakespeare later immortalized. During Britain's first millennia, there were two high points: when the leaders of Britain—first the brothers Belinus and Brennius and then, centuries later, Maximianus—conducted successful imperial wars against Rome. Yet Geoffrey makes no bones about the darker outcomes of British imperial ambition. Belinus leaves his brother Brennius in Rome, where he becomes a vicious tyrant, and Maximianus depopulates the nobility of Britain during his campaign and then abandons Britain only to meet his death in Rome, leaving the realm defenseless without any warriors. Early on, Geoffrey's foundational history thus betrays a profound ambivalence about the costs that underlie its own epic foundationalism.

The stakes of this ambivalence are raised in the second half of Geoffrey's history, in which Arthur emerges as the greatest British king of all time, the ruler of a court where chivalric virtue becomes an ennobling way of life. True to his bellicose ancestors, Geoffrey's Arthur establishes his rule by conquest. Geoffrey depicts him first fighting off the invading Saxons in the battle of Badon Hill and its aftermath, subduing both Scotland and Ireland, and then conquering Norway, Denmark, and Gaul (France and Germany). At that point Arthur halts, recoups, and holds a splendid plenary court at Caerleon, the Roman City of Legions, in Wales. Geoffrey's description of this court—a pinnacle of courteous behavior, chivalric deeds, and ennobling love between knights and ladies—fired the imaginations of subsequent writers; it is here that the Arthur of medieval romance is born.

Yet in Geoffrey, Arthurian courtliness is indeed a brief and shining moment within Britain's longer, darker history of foundational crisis. Arthur's court is no sooner born than its end is foreshadowed. As

Arthur sits at his plenary feast, an embassy from Rome interrupts him and fiercely demands Arthur's submission and tribute. Arthur and his knights decide to match the deeds of their forebears Maximianus and Belinus and conquer Rome instead. A ferocious, triumphant campaign follows, but just as Arthur is about to cross the mountains to take Rome itself, he receives word that his nephew Mordred, left as regent in Britain, has seized his kingdom and besieged his queen, Guenevere. Arthur rushes home and succeeds in quelling Mordred but dies himself, as do most of his knights (including his nephew Gawain). The rest of Geoffrey's history depicts the desperate devolutions of British self-governance. The Saxons return, this time irresistibly, and finally the last British kings are defeated and driven to the remotest corners of the realm to become the Welsh, and Britain passes to the Anglo-Saxons. Thus, Geoffrey's *Historia* at once invents Arthur as the greatest British king and embeds him in a cycle of foundational instability and doom. Arthur is simultaneously an inspiring sovereign whose court can model the best ideals of noble behavior and a conqueror whose ambition impels him to overextend his resources, leading to strife in the royal family and court and then civil turmoil for the realm at large. The *Gawain*-poet recalls this ambivalence when he sums up the history of British kingship as a relentless alternation of "bliss and blunder" (l. 18).

Geoffrey's history has been read as a political justification for the Norman regime of his day and their ongoing territorial expansions into Wales as well as for their campaigns against the Scots and the Irish. Yet several have pointed out that Welsh writers who resisted the Norman expansion and denied Geoffrey's depiction of Welsh devolution still found plenty in Geoffrey that was useful for their own protonationalist histories and stories. Geoffrey's *Historia* was quickly translated into Welsh so that they could make better use of it. Indeed, perhaps because of its ambivalences, the *Historia* was incredibly influential and popular, despite the fact that none of Geoffrey's contemporaries could verify his sources. Gerald of Wales even accuses Geoffrey of weaving such a fabric of historical lies that it attracts hundreds of tiny demons to its manuscript to cluster about the visionary monk who is reading it. Yet even Gerald accepted the shape Geoffrey gave British history, and he drew on it in his own writings about the Welsh and the Irish. Despite the initial doubts about Geoffrey's account from near contemporaries such as William of Newburgh and Gerald of Wales, Geoffrey's history was soon not only accepted as historically authoritative but was also tremendously popular. Writers who were less interested in the long view of ancient British history also made excellent use of Geoffrey's material. Geoffrey's *Historia,* written in Latin prose, was completed before 1139. By 1155, another Anglo-Norman, the poet Wace, had translated it into French verse as the *Roman de Brut.* Wace was fascinated by Geoffrey's Arthur, and he expanded the period covered by Arthur's plenary court from the days it occupied in Geoffrey's narrative to twelve years. Suddenly the brief and shining moment that eventually became known as Camelot was a little less brief. Wace also invented the Round Table and named Arthur's sword Excalibur.

Geoffrey and Wace thus elaborate the idea of Arthur not just as a conqueror but also as a civil leader who fostered a court culture that was a fellowship of idealized knights and a gold standard for ideas of nobility. Hundreds of subsequent medieval writers seized on Wace's expansion of Arthur's court and expanded it further, interpolating shorter stories of Arthur's deeds and the deeds of his knights. They wrote in a variety of languages, Anglo-Norman (the dialect of French that was spoken in England), French, Old High German, and Middle English. Arthurian highpoints in French include the romances of Chrétien de Troyes, Marie de France's *Lanval, The Quest of the Holy Grail,* the *Roman de Silence,* and *Perlesvaus.* In German, Wolfram von Eschenbach's *Parzival* is key. In Britain, there are numerous British histories and romances (many of which bear the name Brut) as well as translations of many of the French Arthurian tales and the dark and epic *Alliterative Morte Arthur.* As more and more people wrote about them, tales of Arthur and other characters from Geoffrey's *Historia,* as well as tales deriving from other British story cycle traditions—such as King Mark of Cornwall and the love of Tristan and the Irish princess Isolde—spread across Britain and Europe. They became collectively known as the Matter of Britain. France and Britain, in particular, developed extensive Arthurian cycles, and the *Gawain*-poet read them and drew on them. *Sir Gawain and the Green Knight* holds a proud place in the canon of Arthurian texts of the Middle Ages; its structural artistry, poetic beauty, and subtle questioning of the conceptual underpinnings of Arthurian writing place it at the apex of Arthurian writing in Middle English.

Literary Contexts: Medieval Romance

The *Gawain*-poet chose to write his poem as a romance, and he clearly knew the genre well. Romance was the most widespread and popular nondevotional literary genre of the Middle Ages. Medieval romances, as opposed to modern romantic love stories, narrated the deeds of a central, usually noble person and his or her relationship to courtly society or the life of the realm more generally. Romances are highly conventionalized, featuring stock characters such as young male knights-in-the-making, fair ladies who motivate or endanger the romance hero, courtly monarchs with whom the knights must gain some accommodation, and a variety of challengers and enemies. When the *Gawain*-poet chooses just five central characters for his poem—Gawain the hero, King Arthur, the challenging Green Knight, the beautiful Lady, and the shadowy Morgan—he is distilling a typical romance down to its essential moving elements to examine and reimagine them.

Sir Gawain and the Green Knight draws on both insular British and Continental romance traditions, revealing a poet intimately familiar with a wide range of Arthurian and romance texts. British and Continental romances developed different depictions of Arthur's court in a regional tug of war between rival literary traditions. In the British romances that follow and build on Geoffrey of Monmouth's twelfth-century reinvention of Arthur in his *Historia* (c.1137), Arthur is often an energetic world conqueror. His greatest knights are his immediate relatives, including his nephew, Gawain, and they are British. By contrast, in many Continental romances Arthur is a passive figurehead. He sits at court while his knights go out on quest and do great deeds in his name and for their own betterment. In many Continental, French, and German texts, the most illustrious of Arthur's knights, such as Lancelot, Bors, and Parzival, are foreign to Arthur's court. Gawain is treated neutrally in earlier French works, such as Chrétien de Troyes' *Erec et Enide*, *Le Chevalier au Lion*, *Le Chevalier de la Charrete*, and *Percival* (c.1160–1180) and Marie de

France's *Lanval* (c.1170–1180). These romances make Gawain a pinnacle of chivalry at Arthur's court but often consign him to an offstage B-plot and dramatize his inability to solve the problem facing the hero. Later works denigrate Gawain and the other British magnates as chivalric also-rans or even actively despicable next to virtuosi like Lancelot.

In many Continental romances, Gawain becomes famous as a knight who slips all too easily into amusing but sometimes dishonorable sexual misadventures. The parodic *Chevalier à l'Epée* (*Knight of the Sword*) has so many parallels with *Sir Gawain and the Green Knight* that it is difficult to believe that the *Gawain*-poet did not know of it. Like *Gawain,* it features a gorgeous estate with a mysterious host and a beautiful lady who becomes the host's cat's-paw to test Gawain's virtue. At its center, Gawain and the Lady are thrown into bed together, and Gawain is tempted to make love to her. He is kept from doing so by the threat of a monstrous self-wielding sword over the bed, but he tries to kiss her anyway, deciding it is "better to die with honor than live with shame"—as he would were it ever to be known that he had slept next to a beautiful woman without demonstrating his prowess. The sword leaves him alive but gives him a slight wound, which paradoxically proves him to be the best knight in the world, because none of his predecessors had survived its blow. The *Chevalier à l'Epée* parodies the conventions of medieval romance in a way that resonates with *Sir Gawain and the Green Knight*'s more serious questions about knightly honor and shame.

Sir Gawain and the Green Knight follows British Arthurian traditions in making Gawain the pinnacle of chivalry at Arthur's court and the hero of the romance. Yet it also draws on Continental traditions when it allows Arthur to recede into the background, and in parts 2 and 3 it foregrounds Gawain's reputation as a peerless lover whose amorous exploits have created a well-documented reputation for love-talking and courteous behavior. The Green Knight and the Lady measure Gawain by his literary reputation across both traditions. Whenever Gawain seems to flag, they lash him with challenges to his very identity: Would Gawain ever deny a kiss to a beautiful, willing lady? Would Gawain ever flinch from a blow? Is he really Gawain? If he is not, who else can he be? And anxiously, obediently, his right to his own identity on the line, Gawain kisses the Lady and stands fast for the axe. Gawain, as a result, emerges as a fairly neurotic hero, leading his life on a chivalric high wire. The *Gawain*-poet thus subjects his version of Gawain to the literary expectations created by other romance writers. This enables him to create a hero caught up in the anxieties of maintaining his literary reputation as the best knight (and courtly lover) in the realm. And as the poet explores the vulnerabilities of his hero, he is able to reflect on larger facets of medieval romance traditions—their ideological investments in aristocratic social systems of honor, shame, masculinity, and class privilege.

Social Contexts: Fourteenth-Century England

Fourteenth-century England was a feudal monarchy, but one that was unusually centralized by European standards. Government consisted of a king with his administrative apparatus and a parliament divided, after 1341, into the upper House of Lords, where the greater nobility and clergy of the realm could pursue their interests, and the lower House of Commons, where knights, members of the lower gentry, and burgesses—influential merchants representing the civic interests of major towns and cities—could represent their own constituencies and pursue their aims. However, the vast majority of the population, the laboring classes, went unrepresented in Parliament and had to sue for change at the local level, if at all, in the manorial and village courts, which were run by members of the local gentry and civil justices of the peace commissioned by the king.

Medieval social theorists often describe feudal societies as comprising three estates: fighters, prayers, and workers—each of which supported the other two in a task necessary for the common good. By the fourteenth century, however, this description could no longer account for the complexity of the social structure because each estate spanned such a wide range of status levels and occupations. The civil rulers—the monarchy, nobility, and gentry—were trained to varying degrees in war, high culture, and administration and ranged from the greatest barons of the realm to the least provincial knights. Ambitious but indigent knights often joined hands with the nebulous, not-quite-aristocratic gentry class, which comprised esquires and well-placed retainers in service to noblemen. These members of the lower nobility and gentry were continually on the lookout for means of advancing themselves—through lucrative military contracts, aristocratic service, or mercantile trade and speculation in partnership with merchants in the cities.

The ecclesiastical estate was similarly broad in scope; church officials had their own hierarchy: from archbishop, to bishop, to archdeacon, right down to the local parish priest, who might be a peasant. It also included a collection of clerics who were trained in cathedral schools or at universities but had not yet been ordained, or taken major orders, and often served in bureaucratic posts at every social level. As noted above, the *Gawain*-poet may have come from this class. In addition there were members of ancient well-endowed monastic orders, such as the Benedictines, which included both literate monks who sometimes claimed aristocratic status and the less literate lay brothers, who did the manual work in monasteries. There were also members of the fraternal orders, Franciscan, Carmelite, and Dominican friars, who were given particular boundaries within which they could preach, raise funds, and hear confession, but often were in competition with priests and ecclesiastical functionaries for support within local parishes.

The estate of workers was where the three-estates model was least helpful because it comprised such a large population and range of status levels, social locations, and occupations. In the countryside, there were peasants, agricultural workers who could be serfs bound to a piece of land or free laborers able to move from place to place contracting for work. Some peasants were seasonal laborers, scrabbling for a living from year to year, whereas others were prosperous, living in their own houses in villages, owning land, and participating in local government. Others followed a trade: blacksmiths, millers, coopers, butchers, and colliers. Women's work was integrated into the village economy, and women functioned as alewives, cooks, spinners, weavers, and clothiers as well as domestic laborers. In cities, laborers included odd-jobbing noncitizens, local grocers, tradesmen, artisans, and prosperous merchants trading in wine, luxury goods, or wool—fourteenth-century England's most valuable export. Livelihoods in the largest towns and cities were organized into craft guilds with their own hierarchy, from indentured apprentices, to journeymen, to guild masters. Guild masters could live like princes, participating in city and parliamentary government; the mayor was elected from their ranks.

Towns were also places of educational labor, from parish schools, to cathedral schools, to the already multiplying colleges in Oxford and Cambridge, to the Inns of Court in London, where lawyers trained. Clerks in training played a lively part in town life, especially in university towns such as Oxford and Cambridge, but they also found positions as accountants within guilds. Outside towns, clerks were useful adjuncts on manorial estates, as accountants, secretaries, and private chaplains. It is a manorial estate that Gawain stumbles on in the second part of the poem when he arrives at the lord's house—and *Sir Gawain and the Green Knight* explores the experience of life in a prosperous manor, with its porter and servitors, public hall and private chambers, and well-tended game park.

Fourteenth-century English society had its origins in a feudal political organization. Feudal government is a way of delegating power and dispersing rule to the local level, while maintaining a hierarchized social order, and it is an effective form of government when centralized administrations are unable to muster their own enforcement apparatus (such as a permanent police force and standing army). Traditionally, feudal society had been bound by exchanges of oaths of service, fealty, and mutual support up and down the chain of society: between the king and his greater barons; the barons and the aristocracy; the aristocracy and the local gentry; the gentry and the local peasantry; and finally (although figuratively) between the peasantry and the land itself. (The peasants, after all, worked the land whose tilth was the basis of the whole feudal economy.) By the fourteenth century, however, English feudalism had already been thoroughly penetrated by the growth of a money economy, with contracts and retention fees coinciding with or replacing exchanges of goods and services. Historians call it "bastard feudalism."

In addition, three major events made fourteenth-century England a time of unprecedented social mobility and change: the Black Death, the Hundred Years' War, and the Rising of 1381—all of which probably occurred in the *Gawain*-poet's lifetime. The Black Death, or bubonic plague, was an epidemic caused by the *Yersinia pestis* bacteria and carried by fleas that infected the common black rat. The "huge mortalyte," as it was called at the time, originated in inland

Asia and spread rapidly along the trade systems linking Asia, Europe, and Africa, to strike England in the autumn of 1348. In the next two years it killed between 30 percent and 60 percent of the population and returned to strike again in 1361 and at intervals throughout the fourteenth and fifteenth centuries, with variant strains returning in localized epidemics up to the eighteenth century. Its long-term effect was to reduce the population from between three and seven million to about two million, probably disproportionately among the laboring classes. As a result there was a postplague labor shortage. Wages began to rise in order to compete for the smaller pool of laborers. To an unprecedented extent, workers of all sorts were able to set their own terms and improve their conditions. Many historians see this as the beginning of the rise of the middle class in England. However, inflation began to burden the English economy, and the English government, which had survived the plague in good order, began passing laws to fix wages to preplague levels and control the movement of workers in search of better wages. As early as 1349, Edward III passed the Ordinance of Laborers, but it was ineffective. It was followed in 1351 with the more energetic Statute of Laborers, which not only further depressed wages but also enjoined that all able-bodied men and women work, enforcing imprisonment for idlers and fining any hirer who raised wages above the stipulated levels. The year 1388 brought the Statute of Cambridge, which forbade even free workers to move around the country without legal permission. None of these statutes was effective because they could not be systematically enforced and the preplague wage levels themselves were unsustainable in the new burgeoning economy. However, they increased civil unrest and made the government much more obtrusive at the local level by empowering local justices of the peace to administer unusual fines and enforcements.

At the same time, England was engaged in the Hundred Years' War with France, a war over the French succession that Edward III began in 1337. After ineffective and costly opening salvos the tide of the war turned in England's favor, and the English armies won strategic victories at Crécy (1346), Calais (1347), and Poitiers (1356). In 1360 Edward III signed the treaty of Brétigny, renouncing his claim to the French throne but ensuring the English jurisdiction over almost a fourth of France, including territories in Brittany, Aquitaine, and Ponthieu. Between 1369 and 1389, however, the French fought back and the English steadily lost or conceded many of those territories, waging expensive campaigns, which were supported by increased English taxation. In 1377, John of Gaunt, the king's uncle, petitioned for a new domestic tax to support the war in France. This was a flat-rate poll tax, levied on more than half the population of England, regardless of status or income, and it was levied again in slightly different terms in 1379 and 1381. In 1381, the tax demanded a shilling (a fairly large amount of money) from everyone in the realm over the age of fifteen.

This unusually heavy war taxation combined with ongoing resistance to the Statute of Laborers and the new, energetic postplague labor market to provoke an unprecedented popular rebellion, the Rising of 1381, also known as the Peasants' Revolt, although many nonpeasants, landowners, civic artisans, and disenfranchised laborers joined the insurgency. In late May and early June in the county of Essex, east of London, attempts to collect the poll tax sparked a resistance among villagers led by Thomas Baker, a landowner. When a justice was sent to investigate the incident, he was attacked. The rebellion soon spread to the neighboring county of Kent, and in June, parties of insurgents led by Wat Tyler marched on London. There the city gates were opened to them by parties of civic insurgents, and the rebels proceeded not to inflict general mayhem but rather to attack precise targets—the richest nobles and ecclesiasts of the realm. The insurgents burned Savoy Palace, the residence of the king's uncle, John of Gaunt, the most powerful magnate in the realm, but they forbade any looting. They attacked the Tower of London, where they beheaded Archbishop Sudbury, the chief chancellor and the highest prelate in the kingdom, and Robert de Hales, the lord treasurer, and displayed their heads on London Bridge. Artisans and tradesmen in the city took advantage of the disorder to slaughter their business rivals, the licensed Flemish merchants who resided in London.

There is evidence of considerable organization among the insurgents. They had a list of grievances and a political action plan: they wished to abolish lordship, both clerical and secular, while retaining the king as head of newly equitable commonwealth. They presented themselves as righteous defenders of tradition and the rights of the commons—and as rescuers of the king from his bad counselors. They targeted recent charters and written documents that they saw as abrogating their rights and demanded in vain the original charters that had traditionally empowered them—which they called "the Statutes of Winchester," whether they existed or not. On June 12, the eve of their assault on London, according to chroniclers (who were very hostile to the insurgents and slanted their accounts accordingly) John Ball preached a sermon on the theme "When Adam dolve [dug] and Eve span, who was then a gentleman?"—a text that returns to Eden to denaturalize the bases of aristocracy itself.

In London, the insurgents met at Smithfield with the young King Richard II and a party of his nobles, and Wat Tyler, their leader, was killed by one of the king's party, the Lord Mayor of London. In the confusion following Tyler's fall, the king was able to exploit the insurgents' faith in his leadership; according to chroniclers he rode toward the gathered insurgents and instructed them to follow him, promising them that their demands would be granted, that Tyler had been knighted, and that Tyler would join them at Miles End, a much less defensible location. There they were corralled and dispersed by the king's militia, and in the subsequent weeks their other leaders were killed. The revolt left a deep scar in the society of the realm, energizing the fears of both the powerful and the conservative and lingering in the memory of the gentry. There were subsequent popular rebellions (for various causes) in 1400, 1450, and 1549.

The *Gawain*-poet thus lived at a time when traditional feudal structures and values were altering in response to new social and demographic conditions. The dominant ways of thinking that equated the values of the monarchy and aristocracy with the values of England at large were still powerful but no longer as generally credible. Royal and aristocratic control over legislation and taxation were challenged by new voices in the House of Commons and elsewhere. These new voices spoke for the interests of the cities, with their powerful merchants and expanding networks of trade, and the gentry of the countryside, who increasingly exerted their powers as local law enforcement. A more fundamental challenge came from the laborers and artisans of the realm at large, who were alert to opportunities to organize and assert their interests even when traditional channels were inadequate. This caused innovations in legislation and government and sparked new definitions of the common good—by both those in power and their challengers. At the end of the century, the king himself, Richard II, was deposed and killed for exercising too free a hand over the hereditary prerogatives of his greater nobles.

These contemporary challenges to chivalry and monarchical power are addressed in the poem when it stages its major conflict—a test of the right of King Arthur and Gawain, Arthur's proxy, to their reputations as the highest exemplars of chivalry in the realm. The Green Knight repeatedly proposes contractual games with Arthur and Gawain; his games are based on incommensurate exchanges (such as kisses for carcasses) or unworkable ones (such as mortal blows) that underscore both the contingency and the potential manipulability of such short-term arbitrary contracts. In contrast, Gawain holds to his sworn word with a tenacity rooted in the old feudal values of *trawthe* (truth) and unshaken loyalty. This puts him at a considerable disadvantage when dealing with his wily challengers. The poem thus underscores the conflict between traditional chivalric values and contemporary contractual forms of chivalry in order to explore the limits of chivalry in a changing world. How can chivalric exemplarity—the best, most courteous, most devout knight—operate in a courtly sphere of change, opportunism, and opportunity, where traditional forms have been adapted to contingencies and received meanings have been scrutinized and reinterpreted?

Plot and Structure

The plot of *Sir Gawain and the Green Knight* combines two subplots, each centered on an exchange. The outer plot is driven by an exchange of blows and the inner, embedded plot by an exchange of winnings. Both exchanges are framed as games and both exchanges are, on the face of it, strange. They seem to invite Gawain to participate in games he cannot lose, only to develop complications that entrap him into more complicated exchanges. In the opening scene, the Green Knight challenges Arthur and Gawain to a combat game that breaks the rules of combat. Instead of fighting as equals and staging their mutual skills, one contestant administers a blow that the other has to endure without defending himself—a potentially fatal game when the weapon in question is the Green Knight's enormous glittering axe. The second game is seemingly less threatening but equally bizarre. The lord will go hunting while Gawain sleeps late and stays indoors, recovering from his journey and amusing himself with the noble ladies at home. At the end of the day, they will gift each other with whatever each has gained. These exchanges at first seem very tempting—whoever strikes the first blow has a clear advantage, and whoever goes out actively hunting clearly stands to win (and give up) more than a person who stays inside and sleeps late. Yet each game tempts Gawain with an easy conclusion in order to involve him in a much more serious test. Will he keep his word when his life and honor are publicly on the line? Will he also keep it in trivial matters that are kept secret?

The exchange of blows game occupies the first and the fourth part of the poem and—by way of two of the most beautiful and chilling journeys in medieval poetry—takes Gawain from the festive security of Arthur's court to the desolate peril of the Green Chapel. The exchange of winnings game takes up the end of the second part and the third part of the poem; it seems to restore Gawain to the familiar comforts of a distant but very hospitable court, where he can relax and recover from the ardors of his journey and celebrate Christmas. However, the aura of relaxation and familiarity is deceptive, and Gawain finds his most perilous engagements where he least expects them—cozy in his bed.

The contrasts between the two games and their venues create dynamic tension in the poem between the external frame plot and nested interior plot and raise larger questions about how exteriors and interiors relate to each other. The poem leads the reader to expect that the two plot-games are unrelated—the lord's castle is just a diversion from Gawain's real journey toward the Green Chapel—yet we find out by the poem's end that the two games are inextricable from each other. They test Gawain's loyalty on two fronts, in public and private, and as they do so, their tests complicate simple formulas and codes of behavior by dramatizing how differently they operate in public and in private—especially when public and private cannot be separated. The Green Knight plays the role of antagonist and challenger to Arthur's court to test whether it has the right to its reputation as the greatest court of chivalry in history. The Lady plays the role of temptress and challenger to Gawain's virtue to test whether he deserves his reputation as a skillful and honorable lover, but also ultimately to test his honor: can he keep his promises both to her and to her husband?

At the end, the two plots come together and we see each in a new light. But far from resolving questions about Gawain's virtue, loyalty, and honor, the convergence of the plots creates more problems. Gawain's final interpretation of his adventure—as signifying his covetousness and lack of courage—does not coincide with the Green Knight's kinder interpretation: that Gawain really does deserve his title as the best knight of the land, except that he loves his life a little too much. And neither interpretation fits with the laughing reception of Arthur and his courtiers, who make Gawain's badge of solitary shame into a badge of courtly fellowship and honor. The reader is left to judge among those three divergent interpretations, as the poet begs all the questions he has raised and gracefully ends the poem where it began, with the siege of Troy and a final prayer.

Sir Gawain as Fallible Hero

Throughout the poem, Gawain functions as an audience touchstone. On first reading, the reader is as much in the dark as Gawain concerning the larger implications of the bizarre contracts, occluded intentions, and veiled wordplay that beset the hero. Gawain fulfills his role as the noblest, most exemplary, and most courteous knight of his time by valiantly doing the best that is expected of him at any given moment. Essentially reactive, he is careful to behave according to the conventions of polite society. The narrative itself seems to relish Gawain's passivity: in Part 3, it lingers over the prospect of the lie-abed knight, obeying the lord's instructions by sleeping late, struggling to come up with a new strategy, while the light grows stronger on the walls and the Lady creeps in to pin him down. For Gawain is operating innocently in an unexpected and deceptive world. As Gawain passes from familiar Arthurian territory into some strange places indeed, he encounters unexpected contingencies with a heady combination of chivalric grace and performance anxiety that ultimately creates perceptible strain.

However, in some respects, Gawain takes respect for conventions to such extremes that it becomes a little bizarre. In Part 1, why does he ask—at the critical moment when Arthur is brandishing the axe to engage the blustering challenger—for his uncle's (and Guenevere's) permission to rise from the table and seek council with the king before getting down to his necessary king-saving intervention? After the fireworks of Part 1, why does he spend ten months celebrating the yearly round of festivities at Arthur's court before embarking on his journey to the Green Chapel? Clearly attendance at court was expected of knightly courtiers and members of the king's familiar household. But surely there was also some incentive to getting an early start on his quest for the Green Knight of the Green Chapel (such as lack of a specific destination or name). Other questing knights in Arthurian literature go off on long quests at the slightest provocation, despite their courtly attendance obligations. In fact, Gawain's unusual concern with convention—with doing what is expected of him—accords with the character's reputation as established in the genre of Arthurian romance. French Arthurian romances, in particular, make Gawain the archetypal social animal. He embodies the camaraderie of the court. Although many romances examine their heroes' inner lives to highlight conflicts between individual desire and social expectation, chivalric identity is necessarily a public performance; a knight ultimately mattered only if he could perform his chivalric role at court and be acknowledged, ratified, and commemorated by his peers. Gawain's incessant sociability contrasts with the behavior of such knightly loners as Lancelot, who plays the role of stranger and outsider because it enables better chivalric theater when he comes forward at intervals to vindicate himself. In *Sir Gawain and the Green Knight,* we see how closely Gawain is tied to the company of his fellow courtiers when the poet stages their bitter regret at his leave-taking, his own desolation when he is wandering through the Welsh and Cheshire wildernesses, his joy at finding harborage at the lord's castle, and Arthur's court's delight in welcoming him back, however compromised. By stressing Gawain's extreme reliance on convention and courtly assessment, the poet not only explores a fallibility in his hero but also implicates the chivalric judgment of the court itself. Perhaps neither Arthur nor Gawain are the best judges of character; perhaps better assessments can emerge through the more complex interpretive possibilities that the poem offers its reader.

In creating a character so preoccupied with synthesizing and performing the diverse ideals of knightliness before a company of chivalric peers, the poet implicitly invites questioning about the very possibility of such chivalric perfectionism. But Gawain's exaggerated care for the conventions and the expectations of others—and the depth of his despondency when he falls short—may also suggest more fundamental questions: questions about the limitations and costs of fetishizing ideals and expectations, of obeying so carefully the polite forms that bind together noble society and establish its zones of mutual respect and intelligibility. At what cost comes the adherence to courtly conventions? What has to be sacrificed to be a public paragon of courtesy? What unintended limitations might such conventions impose on those who follow them?

One of the limitations is tactical. Arthur, his courtiers, and Gawain enter the poem as virtual children, in their "fresh youth" (l. 54), or, less respectfully, as the Green Knight taunts them, beardless boys (l. 280). Yet, oddly, young as they are in the poem, their fabulous reputations already exist. It is as though the poet were confronting the youthful court of ancient Camelot with the centuries of literary reputation they had amassed by the fourteenth century. Thus the Arthurian characters, caught by the poem in their "fresh youth" (l. 54), have to struggle to fill their mature shoes—as if, by virtue of being portrayed in earliest adulthood, they are expected to conduct themselves even more ideally than they would have if they had been shown having already acquired full beards. If they fall off even slightly, they cannot be the illustrious characters that everyone in the poem's audience has heard about. In this way, the Green Knight acts like a fourteenth-century reader of the poem who has acquired the power to enter the textual world. He challenges the court, and when the courtiers fail to respond to his challenge at once he immediately begins to taunt them with their achievements:

"Is this Arthur's house?" he thundered at them.
"The retainers they talk of through regions and realms?
Where's your presumption, your pomp, and your pride?
Your gall and your grimness, your grudges and threats?"
(ll. 309–12)

The Green Knight's taunt is successful. Arthur blushes shamefully and becomes enraged, rising instantly to accept the Green Knight's challenge himself, a reaction the Green Knight welcomes. In this scene it is precisely Arthur's attachment to idealized forms—an unbendable code of behavior on the one hand, his own illustrious reputation on the other—that renders him vulnerable to the Green Knight's manipulation.

In addition to tactical problems, moreover, rigid adherence to idealized forms of knightly behavior also begets profound interpretive limitations. Arthur's court is trapped in dichotomous thinking. They render the world meaningful by dividing it—friend or foe, honor or shame, truth or treachery, collectivity or solitude—and clinging to one side while abjuring the other. Yet as a mixture of nature and culture, the Green Knight forces dichotomies together in a way that stymies simple interpretation. How can a green-skinned half-giant dress like a beautifully attired nobleman? He bears no device, declares no family, states no estate. Rather he dangles "my house and my home and my name" (l. 408) as prizes to be awarded at the end of the fatal game rather than prerequisites for the courtly encounter itself.

Thus at the poem's beginning we see Arthur struggling to put the inexplicable Green Knight into a category. Is he there to issue a challenge to battle or is he there as a form of light entertainment before the feast? Is he human or monster? At first, despite the knight's stated challenge to a friendly game, Arthur sees his axe, not his festive garments and holly branch, and responds combatively, "If you crave battle bare, / We'll find you one to fight" (ll. 277–78). Later, however, the "Christmas game" turns nightmare, with the Green Knight's severed head having been kicked around the floor of the hall by flinching courtiers, only to open its eyes and mouth and address Gawain with what seems to be a promise of certain death. Yet Arthur downplays the bloody encounter, dismissing it as a playful diversion, well fitting a Yuletide feast. There seems to be no nuanced interpretation available. From the beginning to the end of their encounter with the Green Knight, Arthur's court is caught in an interpretive quandary that entrances and silences them: "as if sunken in sleep, they slaked all their noise" (l. 244). Yet the problem is more than just Arthur —the idealizing and dichotomizing reflexes of romance itself as a genre are on the line as well. In effect the *Gawain*-poet uses characters within a genre to question the cognitive presuppositions of that genre. At question are courtly romance habits of organizing the world. Readers are left to supply the interpretive flexibility that Arthur's court lacks and deal with the quandary of the Green Knight with whatever resources they can muster.

At the poem's end and driven by his failure, we see Gawain himself still taking refuge in this kind of black-and-white thinking. To Gawain, honor cannot coexist with shame—so if Gawain can no longer encapsulate the pentangle as the epitome of honor, he has to wear the girdle as an emblem of shame. Dichotomous thinking is a necessary tool that does a great deal of tactical social work in rendering the world meaningful, and indeed at the poem's beginning, readers themselves are as ill equipped to figure out the Green Knight as are Arthur and his courtiers. But to a reader who has been drawn in and kept guessing by the poem's brilliant, urgent, contradictory emplotments, the poem in all its detail and complexity becomes a training in subtlety. By the time we reach the final scenes, Gawain's thinking has come to seem retrograde—as though Gawain were retreating, wounded, into a smaller, safer world than the one into which the poem has led its readers.

Matters of Life and Death

So what kind of world does the poem open for its readers that its protagonist cannot step into? The poem's beginning has swept us into a historical landscape that ties together dichotomies where truth and treachery, bliss and blunder, brutality and civilization are bound together and sweep in a dizzying succession across time. But from its first lines, the poem complicates cognitive oppositions with unnerving associations. It repeatedly urges us not to see only one side or the other but rather to notice (and admire) an interplay (or painful embattlement) of both. Subsequent descriptions of the experience of time follow this same pattern, linking unlike things together because they succeed each other in human experience. And this violent forcing together of unlike things over time creates both drama and beauty in the poem. It constitutes the poem's most distinctive and effective aesthetic habit.

One of the loveliest passages of the poem entices readers to experience the tensions of these contrasting associations by depicting the passage of the year as successive battles between warring seasons:

A year slides by swiftly, never the same,
And the early days seldom accord with the end.
Yuletide soon yielded to the rest of the year,   500
With the sequence of seasons ensuing by turns.
Christmas must cede to cold comfort in Lent.
Lent flays our flesh with fish and plain fare.
But then the world-weather quarrels with winter.
Cold unclasps its clamps as the clouds lift on high.   505
The fair rain falls rustling in fruitful warm showers,
Plying soft plains. Flowers appear.
Green ground and grove go gowned in new verdure.
Busy birds build and bravely sing out
For soft summer's solace that settles thereafter   510
          on hills.
     And blossoms swell and blow
     By rich hedgerows and rills,
     And notes the wild birds know
     Fill woods with pleasant trills.   515

Then summer itself arrives with soft winds,
When Zephyrus breathes on the seeds and young shoots.
How glad is the green herb that grows from them then,
As the dampening dew drips from its leaves,
To bide there in bliss for bright beams from the sun!   520
But harvest comes hastening and hails him full quickly,
Warns him for winter to wax and grow ripe,
And drives in the drought so that dust rises up
From the face of the fields, flying high in the air.
In the sky the wild winds wrestle the sun.   525
Leaves drop from the linden and light on the ground,
The grass turns to gray that was green at first,
And all ripens and rots that had risen in spring.
And so the year turns, on yesterdays many.

Winter waxes again as the world says it must,   530
        no jest. (ll. 498–531)

This sweeping passage, composed as a chain of arresting tactile, visual, and emotional images, portrays earthly bodies as subjected to that onrush of time—by turns pleasurable and painful—that corresponds to the seasons. After all the racket and feasting of Yuletide in Part 1, the poet gives the hunger of "crabbed" Lent disagreeable claws that probe and clench in the deprived bodies of the penitent. Yet before another line, a contentious spring enters to dispute winter's harshness and the chill air shrinks down in surrender before it, while "clouds lift" almost with a perceptible sigh of relief. The showers of rain that fall are wonderfully warm, and we identify with the growing things of the ground and the groves as they unfurl and stretch into the bliss of a growing summer. The gentle west winds ease the plants into joyous growth, waiting for the moistening dew to drop on them and the sun to blush them with pleasure. But the passing of time brings harsher experiences as the year wanes. A cautionary autumn approaches, warning the "green herbs" that they had better hurry up and ripen. Battle is joined once more in the heavens as the droughts of late summer give way to the winds of autumn in a whirl of rising dust. Suddenly every growing thing aches with mortality. The leaves fly down and the grass becomes gray, and ripening begins to edge toward rotting and the desolation of winter.

The year's dizzying turn from the immediacy of these experiences to a litany of yesterdays is well summed up in the echoing of the verb *yerning*, a pun. In the original Middle English text, the passage begins with, "A year yernes ful yerne, and yeldez neuer lyke" (l. 498) and culminates with "And thus yirnez the yere in yisterdayez mony" (l. 529). *Yerning* means "hastening," "passing" but also "longing," "wishing," "desiring." In this passage, there is nothing to do but feel time acutely—and thus the passage of the year constitutes a sentimental education in life and death. This is simply how time passes, the poet says, "no jest." It is something you cannot get away from.

The rest of the poem incessantly dramatizes similar juxtapositions between life and death, beginnings and endings, and pleasure and pain. In Part 2, Gawain's desolate journey in search of the Green

Chapel lands him in a wilderness where monsters beset him, and winter is the worst monster of all. Yet the minute he prays to Mary for safe harborage to celebrate Christmas, the lord's wonderful castle shimmers into view through the trees and he is received into the comforts of a court that rivals Arthur's in its genteel hospitality. In Part 3, the poem hops back and forth between death in the forest and love-speech in the bedchamber with whiplash-inducing speed and dexterity. When the Lady enters the poem as a vision of youthful beauty, she comes hand in hand with an old woman who epitomizes ancient ugliness—and the poet interweaves their descriptions until we scarcely know if we should goggle or flinch. On the last day of Gawain's stay at the lord's castle, he dreams darkly about his coming encounter with the Green Knight—and is startled awake by the sight of the Lady opening the window onto the bright morning. Her beauty signifies nothing less than the life he is afraid of losing, and his fear intensifies the dangerous pleasure of their last conversation. When the poem's ending finally comes, and we are left with the three divergent interpretations of Gawain's adventure—fatal flaw, honorable accolade, and bonding experience—the reader experiences the last instance of sudden sharp contrast in a poem that seems to delight in inducing such interpretive vertigo.

This aesthetic habit of forcing interpretive uncertainty not only offers opportunities for exquisite poetry but also allows the poet to alert the reader to the possible connections between these sudden contrasts. In Part 2, is the lord's castle such a refuge from danger after all? In Part 3, how does the lord's hunt in the forest correspond to the lady's hunt in the bedroom? How do the hunted animals' tactics correspond to Gawain's? Are the old lady and the young one related more fundamentally than the contrast between them suggests? We find out at the end that they are. Even at the largest level of the poem's two juxtaposed plot-games, what does the fatal exchange of blows game have to do with the festive exchange of winnings game? In every case the poem seduces us with contrasts within the poem's world only to suggest unexpected affinities.

A Liturgical Framework in King Arthur's Court

One of the poem's most subtle juxtapositions is the way it layers medieval religious practices into noble life, and nowhere is this more resonant than in the liturgical calendar, whose feasts frame crucial events in the narrative. Advent, Christmas, and the Feast of the Circumcision on New Year's Day are its high points. The Green Knight interrupts Arthur's Yuletide festivities like a spirit of regeneration in the midst of winter. The poem begins on New Year's Day, which in medieval celebrations of the Christmas season was the day allotted for gift giving—and the Green Knight does leave his beautiful, deadly axe as a gift to the knight who accepts his challenge. Gawain sets out on his journey to the Green Chapel on November 2, the Feast of All Souls, which as a day for commemorating all the faithful departed is an appropriate day to set out on his own journey toward a seemingly certain, but faith-keeping death. He prays to Mary for harborage on Christmas Eve day—the anniversary of her own need for shelter at Bethlehem—and she answers his prayer in the instantaneous appearance of the lord's castle. Gawain celebrates Christmas, the feast of the Nativity, feasting and merrymaking with the lord, and the celebrations continue through the next two days, the feasts of St. Stephen and St. John the Evangelist. The feast of the Holy Innocents, commemorating the children slaughtered by Herod, is silently elided; a day seems actually left out of the poem's calendar and narration—no one knows why—yielding to the last three days of the year. This time of Gawain's testing includes the feast of St. Thomas Becket of Canterbury on December 29 and St. Sylvester on December 31. Finally, Gawain sets out on the last leg of his journey to the Green Chapel on New Year's morning, the Feast of the Circumcision, also called the feast of the New Man or the New Name, which liturgically commemorates the completion of the Jewish holy law and its transformation into the Christian law. It also recalls the remaking of the Christian soul in Christ in a spiritual circumcision and its entry into a devout Christian community—and Gawain does receive a transformative cut on his neck (although not one he welcomes) and returns to his loving community in Arthur's court, however isolated in penance he feels among them.

The Christian calendrical frame considerably complicates the task of interpreting the poem. With what degree of authority are we to invest the poem's religious template? Is it there to illuminate or satirize the worldly ways of the ancient nobility? Has religious practice been so thoroughly incorporated into gentility that there is no tension between them whatsoever? How should we understand Gawain's failing? Did he prove lacking in faith or in loyalty, or both?

The poet, with characteristic subtlety, does not press any point or invite any judgment, even when one seems called for. In fact, while withholding narratorial judgment, he accentuates the question of judgment by invoking powerful penitential and chivalric ritual frameworks for testing and transformation. For instance, he fills the last part of the narrative with resonances of the medieval sacrament of confession, which was one of the seven sacraments required of the faithful as part of the larger practice of penance and the return of sinners to God and the community of the church. Impelled by the contrition in their hearts, sinners were to confess their sins to a priest by mouth and perform satisfaction—through asceticism, redress, prayer, and penance—in order to receive absolution from their sin. On the eve of Gawain's fateful journey to the Green Chapel, the knight fittingly makes a formal confession to the lord's chaplain. But what did he confess? Did Gawain mention the Lady's love-token, not yet yielded to the lord according to the compact of their game? Is cheating in a game a sin? Or is the sin his accepting the lace in the first place and trusting to magic rather than faith? The poet respects the confessional seal and tells us nothing of what Gawain actually said—only that he made a full and complete confession and was absolved. Later, Gawain finds himself again confessing to the Green Knight himself. He confesses to cowardice and covetousness—the first a violation of the chivalric code, the second a Christian sin—which the Green Knight indulgently recharacterizes as a slightly excessive love of life and half-mockingly absolves, an absolution that Gawain rejects.

To complicate matters further, his final scene is not simply confessional. It also dramatizes chivalric ritual, especially knightly investiture, the rite of passage that turns a squire into a knight. Gawain kneels, receives a blow from a mature chivalric authority, and finds his chivalric virtue ratified and his understandable fault assessed and excused in chivalric terms (to value one's life and not to spend it rashly are knightly virtues). He is also addressed by the Green Knight for the first time in the poem by his full knightly title: "Sir Gawain."

In fact, both rituals are strikingly ineffective. After confessing to the Green Knight, far from feeling absolved, Gawain feels that he is beyond absolution and must go on confessing his sin forever; he confesses yet again when he returns to Arthur's court. As a knight, Gawain also feels that he has not demonstrated but lost his chivalric honor and, even after his return to Camelot, that he has not gained acceptance into the community but rather become an outcast. Furthermore, to take either of these ritual templates as authoritative is to accord the Green Knight a sacramental, chivalric status from which his own confession of being "Morgan the Goddess'" queen-assassinating cat's-paw disqualifies him. It cannot be an accident that the romance deploys a bizarrely extratextual narrative maneuver, the Arthurian cliché of the Morgan plot, at precisely the moment when it tempts us to accord the most ritual authority portrayed in the poem —that of knightly confessor—to its semisupernatural challenger. The poem deliberately deepens the contrast between the Green Knight as supreme chivalric and spiritual authority on the one hand and, on the other, as a deeply suspicious thoroughly feminized character who panders to Morgan's desires by pandering out his Lady. Thus, while both confession and knightly investiture are at work in this final scene, they only intensify the questions it raises.

Two Important Symbols

The poem's most resonant contrast—and shrewdest association—is its juxtaposition of the two heraldic symbols that Gawain wears to signify his identity: the pentangle and the lace, the endless knot and the double-ended knot. Gawain's evolution from a perfect but un-tried hero to a hero flawed by human error could be summed up as a journey from one to the other. In Part 2 of the poem, Gawain prepares for his dangerous journey by arming himself and taking up the shield that bears his personal symbol. The pentangle sums up Gawain's identity as an ideal knight and signals it to his fellow knights. As befits an ideal knight, the pentangle is an ideal, abstract form, an interlaced five-pointed star. Yet the allegory of the pentangle as a consummation of twenty-five chivalric virtues in Part 2 seems more an exercise in allegoresis than a compelling poetic figure. Some of these virtues are corporeal: the five fingers that signify a knight's power to act in the world. Some of them are cognitive: the five senses through which the world informs the body. Some are devotional: the commemorated joys and sorrows of the Virgin that bring religious contemplation closer to human sympathy. Finally some are behavioral: the chivalric virtues practiced by a good knight, including freedom, friendship, cleanness, courtesy, and pity (ll. 652–54). The many virtues that are brought together in the points of the star are tremendously different—as different as a finger, from a joy, from a sorrow, from a sense, and from a virtue—yet the points of the star all look the same. This suggests both the artistry and the arbitrariness of the poet's explanation. The pentangle is also a static symbol—the star never changes—and its very stasis limits application. Is it possible to enact the pentangle virtues all together and at all times? Is it possible wholly to incarnate the pentangle—to embody the faithfulness it represents? Throughout the poem we see Gawain negotiate double binds of loyalty, honor, and courtesy with which the pentangle cannot help him.

But the pentangle is not alone in the poem's symbolic register. Gawain adopts a subsequent token for his knightly insignia when, in Part 4, he wraps himself with the girdle or lace. At first he wears it secretly, beneath his surcoat. Later, he wears it publicly, sashwise, from shoulder to waist across his surcote—which would probably at that time have been embroidered with the pentangle as well—so at the poem's end, when he presents himself to Arthur's court, his emblem would look like a pentangle slashed across by the lace. In contrast to the pentangle, the lace is quite elusive as a symbol. It means different things depending on who is holding it and describing it, and as it passes from hand to hand, it accumulates new meanings. It functions by turns as a love-token, a lady's undergarment, a husband's gift, a precious treasure, Gawain's ace in the hole, a magical device, a commemoration of valor, a badge of shame, and a sign of fellowship. Where the pentangle is static, endless, and closed, the lace is mutable, open-ended, and tied anew every time Gawain wears it. Even though Gawain claims it as a uniquely personal penance, it can equally be adopted by everyone in Arthur's court, as the poem's last scene demonstrates. Ultimately its power comes from its everyday use, not its idealism. The poet thus subverts the interpretive idealism of the pentangle by playing on the continual reinterpretation of the lace. Objects, words, utterances, and poems themselves acquire meaning in the world because they are deployed communally and unpredictably in new contexts. The lace is a much more uncomfortable, ethically challenging badge than the pentangle. Yet perhaps it ends by being "truer" than the pentangle, because it wears its knot visibly rather than claiming perfect and "endless" ideals.

An Outtrage Awenture of Arthurez Wonderez

Sir Gawain and the Green Knight continually confronts readers with paradoxes—events and personages that transgress against expectation or simple interpretation. The poet at the beginning beguiles his audience with a story "that men have held one of the oddest on earth, / A marvel unmatched among all Arthur's wonders" (ll. 28–29). The Middle English adjective the poet applies to his poem is *outtrage,* a cognate of Modern English *outrageous. Outtrage* has a wide semantic range in Middle English: "extravagant," "exalted," "wanton," "wicked," "out of control," "egregious," "bizarre," and "extraordinary." Much in the poem is unaccountable but provocative: the Green Knight's beauty amid his threat, the Lady's threat amid her beauty, the lord's predatory gamesmanship amid his indulgent hospitality, the secret, seductive kisses that Gawain dutifully receives from the wife and transfers to her husband "with all the sweetness and savor that he could supply" (l. 1937). Even if those provocations seem irresolvable, they have an impact in the poem—they incite both wonder and questions. What would have happened if Gawain had been able to swallow his humiliation and return to Bertilak's house to celebrate New Year? Or if Gawain had been seduced by the Lady—would he have kept his compact with the lord by making love to him in his hall? Scholars have argued that the homoerotic possibilities with which the text flirts are there precisely in order that they should be closed again, to return us to a world where only heterosexuality makes sense. And yet—the narrative relishes the masculine beauty of the Green Knight's body and clothing with the same exuberance it does the Lady's gorgeous form, wit, and seductive words.

Ultimately, *Sir Gawain and the Green Knight* invites us to enjoy the interpretive vertigo that ensues when we loosen our grip on the dichotomies we find most secure and explanatory and see the underlying associations between their oppositions, the nuances that complicate their interplay. People cannot be divided neatly into absolute friends and enemies; everyone who is not for a person, a cause, a country need not be against them; thinking otherwise can have grave consequences. The Green Knight is both a friend and an enemy to Gawain. Acts may be necessary compromises rather than betokening only honor or shame. The poem shows repeatedly that truth and treachery, bliss and blunder may coexist and join hands. Absolute dichotomies may give a clear shape to the world, the self, and even the devil. However, they also do work in the world that is interpretively reductive and thus questionable. If the poem's mystery has an ethical purpose, that questioning offers the only way toward it.

Translator's Preface

The Nature of the Poem

From my first encounter with it in graduate school, *Sir Gawain and the Green Knight* has held a special place in my affections. Even then, struggling with the poem's unfamiliar language and verse forms, I was sure that here was a masterpiece if ever there was one—a performance not just to be revered, but relished. The anonymous poet's command of style, detail, and pace; his armory of effects; his unpredictable imagination; his keen psychological insights; his artful plotting; and his combination of entertaining narrative and profound themes put him on a plane few have reached, not just in his day but in any place or time. He may have been a provincial writing in the northwest Midlands of England, but except for some gnarly, throat-clearing country language there is nothing provincial about his work. He was a full-fledged European before the word was invented.

And what a challenge for a translator! The *Gawain*-poet seems to have known Virgil, whom he occasionally imitates. He often sounds like Ovid as well, with his fleet historical flashbacks, his multileveled conversations, his wide compassion, even his somewhat mocking fashion sense. He knew Arthurian stories and traditions set in Britain, but, like Malory later, he knew them in large part from the French, whose courtly romances he also echoes.[1] He could describe any detail, from an embroidered silk band to a stinging snow squall, and make you see and feel it. No one could touch his winter scenes until Shakespeare came along, and not even Shakespeare surpassed them. No poet ever created more enigmatic ladies or harder rocks. He is at home in the mind of a hunted deer or fox or even a green shoot drinking in the

---

1. On this point, see Ad Putter, Sir Gawain and the Green Knight *and French Arthurian Romance* (Oxford: Clarendon Press, 1995).

morning dew. And he couples all this with a profound awareness of time, the cycles of history, the seasons, a person's life.

In short, *Gawain* is anything but a typical knight-in-shining-armor romance; it is high entertainment, to be sure, but also the most powerful work of a master poet. While no translation will ever match the original, it has been my great pleasure to try.

The Verse

The Alliterative Lines

Most of *Sir Gawain and the Green Knight* is written in accentual alliterative verse, a largely superseded form but one that still reads very well, although it may take an unaccustomed reader a page or two to settle into it. It is called "accentual" verse because each long line has four accented syllables along with an undetermined number of unaccented ones, and "alliterative" because of the binding force supplied by alliteration—the chiming of repeated consonant sounds at the beginning of certain syllables, generally accented syllables, and generally three to a line.[2] That is very abstract. To see how it works in practice, consider the poem's opening:

> Siþen þe **sege** and þe as**saut** watz **sesed** at **Troye,**
> Þe borȝ **brit**tened and **brent** to **brond**ez and **ask**ez,
> Þe **tulk** þat þe **trammes** of tresoun þer **wroȝt**
> Watz **tried** for his **trich**erie, þe **trew**est on **erthe.** (ll. 1–4)

> *Once the siege and the assault was ceased at Troy,*
> *The city battered and burnt down to brands and ashes,*
> *The man who entangled that town in his treason*
> *Was impeached for his perfidy, the purest on earth.*

The bolded syllables in the original are the ones most readers would accent—or pronounce with greater force than the others around

---

2. Initial vowels are a special situation. All vowel sounds at the beginning of syllables alliterate with all other vowel sounds, and also with *h*, so a line like

> Ay watz **Arthur** þe **hend**est, as **I** haf herde **telle**

is perfectly regular.

them—and the first three accented syllables in each of the lines al-
literate: *sege, saut, sesed; brit, brent, brond; tulk, trammes, tre; tried, trich,
trew.* Each set starts with the same consonant sound.

Those four opening lines represent the alliterative ideal,[3] which is
ultimately based on Germanic and Old English practice.[4] Fortunate-
ly for translators, the *Gawain*-poet frequently wanders well away from
the ideal, as he does in this passage from stanza 2:

Ande quen þis **Bret**ayn watz **bigged** bi þis **burn rych,**
Bolde **bred**den þer**inne, bar**et þat **lof**den,
In **mon**y turned **tyme tene** þat **wroȝ**ten.
Mo **ferl**yes on þis **fold**e han **fall**en here **oft**
Þen in any o**þ**er þat I **wot,** syn **þat** ilk **tyme.** (ll. 20–24)

Now, since Britain was built by this baron, Lord Brutus,
Brash lads have bred there, bold lovers of battle.
In days that dawned after, they dealt out great dole
Amid portents and prodigies, piled high in this land
Beyond any I've heard of since those olden times.

Here, only the first and third lines hew to the ideal pattern, whereas the
last one has no alliterating accented syllables at all. Although a great deal
of ingenuity has been spent to show that when the *Gawain*-poet's lines
depart from the standard model, they do not *really* depart from the
standard model,[5] the manuscript certainly contains a large number of
lines that look nonstandard without an overlay of special pleading.
Thus, we find examples like these (all from the first two stanzas):

Wel**neȝe** of al þe **wele** in þe **west** iles [first alliterating syllable
     not accented]

3. Or close to it. Strictly speaking, the *t* in *tulk* in l. 3 does not alliterate with the
tr's in *trammes* and *tresoun*, but that is a technicality the *Gawain*-poet com-
monly ignores.
4. Scholars disagree on whether writers of the *Gawain*-poet's generation revived
alliterative verse after some centuries of disuse or whether they drew on an oral
(but unpreserved) tradition still current in their day.
5. See especially Ad Putter, Judith Jefferson, and Myra Stokes, *Studies in the
Metre of Alliterative Verse,* Medium Ævum Monographs, N.S. 25 (Oxford: The
Society for the Study of Medieval Languages and Literature, 2007).

And **neuenes** hit his **aune** nome, as **hit** now **hat** [first accented
   syllable not alliterated][6]
And fer **ou**er þe **French flod Fe**lix **Brut**us [five accented
   syllables]
Þen in any o**þ**er þat I **wot,** syn **þat** ilk **tyme** [almost no
   alliteration in the classic sense]

There are a host of such irregular lines in the poem, and they become
more common as it goes along. Well before the final pages, one finds
stanzas with as many odd lines as regular ones.

   I have likewise allowed myself a good deal of latitude in making
my Modern English version, trying like the poet himself to provide
the distinctive flavor of alliteration but adjusting its intensity when
necessary. Most of my lines have three alliterating syllables, and most
often these are accented. But sometimes, as in the original, fewer or
more than three syllables alliterate or the pattern may include unac-
cented syllables. One particular variation included here is alliterating
the last accented syllable, something the *Gawain*-poet seldom allows,
but that is often necessary to avoid a stilted effect in Modern English.
Consider line 6, where the complement *patrounes* comes before its
verb, *bicome:*

   Þat siþen depreced prouinces, and patrounes bicome
   Welneʒe of al þe wele in þe west iles. (ll. 6–7)

   That afterward conquered provinces and patrons became
   Well nigh of all the wealth in the western iles.

That sort of inversion is rare enough to be distracting today. I have
followed modern word order even though it pulls the final alliterat-
ing syllable to the end of the line:

   Who put down whole provinces to make themselves princes
   Of well nigh all wealth in the isles of the West.

---

6. Note that *aune, hit,* and *hat* form a legitimate sequence. By convention, *h*'s
alliterate with vowel sounds and vowels alliterate with each other.

In this particular instance and many others I tried to put the poetry ahead of hidebound adherence to the alliterative ideal.

The Metrical Lines

Here we are on more familiar ground. Each of *Gawain*'s stanzas ends with a so-called "bob and wheel" written in metrical verse. In the vast majority of cases, the "bob" is grammatically attached to the previous long lines and consists of a single iamb, that is, an unstressed syllable followed by a stressed one. Here is the end of the first stanza:

> *Beyond the French Flood, the lord Felix Brutus*
> *Sets our brave Britain on hills and broad banks,*
> > *full gay.*
> *Where war and wrack and wonder*
> *By turns have each held sway,*
> *And bouts of bliss and blunder*
> *Shift quickly to this day.* (ll. 13–19)

The bob, "full GAY," modifies *Britain* or *banks* in the preceding line (the distinction is not critical) and makes a transition to the rhyming, three-beat lines that follow:

> *Where **war** and **wrack** and **wonder***
> *By **turns** have **each** held **sway**,*
> *And **bouts** of **bliss** and **blunder***
> *Shift **quickly** to this **day**.*

These metrical short lines often contain alliteration, but their rhythm is set by alternating stressed and unstressed syllables and the music of rhyme, which the *Gawain*-poet employs with rare precision for his time. Here as elsewhere he proves himself a master craftsman. His rhymes are lively, unpredictable, and generally exact—no easy achievement when the need for a new rhyme comes up every six syllables.

Translating these pointed and often witty tags was great fun. The poet uses them to comment on the text as he goes, adding summaries, extra detail, historical perspective, foreshadowing, snippets of dialogue, whatever he needs at the moment; and of course they add another touch of complexity to what is already a rich and sophisticated narrative.

They also show, if anyone should doubt it, that here is a writer entirely capable of writing technically correct metrical poetry. His decision to use alliterative verse for the bulk of the poem was deliberate, not something forced on him by his provincial circumstances.

The Poem's Language

The poem's first two lines give a general sense of the poet's language—not just its difficulty, but its range:

> Siþen þe sege and þe assaut watz sesed at Troye,
> Þe borʒ brittened and brent to brondez and askez,

The words with stress in line 1—*sege, assaut, sesed, Troye*—all come from Latin by way of Old French. Those in line 2—*borʒ, brittened, brent,* and *askez*—are native, descended from Old English. In the course of the poem, the writer ranges freely across several registers, venturing into courtly talk—*courtesy, service, romance*—legal terms like "a twelmonyth and a day," church language, and the special vocabularies of foods, fabrics, music, natural scenery, horse-fittings, and, of course, armor and the hunt. He clearly knows a good deal about these subjects and has a rich and exact vocabulary to describe each of them.

But compared to a London writer—Chaucer, say—for all his elegance and sophistication, the *Gawain*-poet is unabashedly northern, and a translation ought to take this into account. Many do not. It is not enough to give the literal sense of his lines. If they are to sound like him, they must contain a relatively high portion of chewy Old English or Norse terms. Here he describes a bristling boar:

> Hef hyʒly þe here, so hetterly he fnast (l. 1587)

Literally, *Heaved highly the [his] hair, so fiercely he snorted. Hef* is just an older spelling of *heaved,* although we probably would not use the word this way today. Nor would we say *hair* for bristles. *Hetterly* and the glorious word *fnast* are no longer part of the language. But we can still come fairly close:

Its hackles rose high, and it grunted so hotly

Hackles and *grunted* are good *Gawain*-like words, both rooted in Old English, while *hotly* is a literal translation of the Middle Low German original of *hetterly*. This is the language of the hunting and outdoor scenes that go far to make *Gawain* so memorable. Here is another example describing that unforgettable second-day chase:

He gete þe bonk at his bak, bigynez to scrape,
Þe froþe femed at his mouth vnfayre bi þe wykez [corners],
Whettez his whyte tuschez. (ll. 1571–73)

He puts his back to a scarp and scrapes out his spot.
An ugly froth foamed at the folds of his mouth
As he whet his white tusks.

Every word of the translation is Germanic—from Old English, West Saxon, or Old Norse. Only *ugly* runs more than one syllable. These lines are as close as I could come to the plainspoken effect as well as the meaning of the poet's Middle English.

In other passages I tried to deal with the challenge of the poem's original language by including French and Latinate words (as the poet did even in vivid action scenes like the beheadings) but playing these off against native and Norse-flavored words. On several occasions the poet imposed a distinct pattern on these intertwined currents of language. The snippet below conveys the court's shock on seeing the Green Knight, before the finer details of his appearance begin to register:

Þer hales in at þe halle dor an aghlich mayster,
On þe most on þe molde on mesure hyghe;
Fro þe swyre to þe swange so sware and so þik,
And his lyndes and his lymes so longe and so grete,
Half etayn in erde I hope þat he were. (ll. 136–140)

. . . through the door hurtled a hair-raising stranger,
The biggest and bulkiest man above ground.

> *From the neck to the waist he was well knit and wide,*
> *And so lusty and long in his loins and his limbs,*
> *He was halfway a giant on earth, by my head.*

The court's horrified amazement accounts for the rustic, unpolished diction—only *mayster* and *mesure* are French. The rest of the words come from Old English or Old Norse.

A few lines later, though, the watchers have somewhat recovered their composure and begin to reassess the intruder in more courtly terms, noting—to take some of the sting out of his strangeness—that he wears

> A strayte cote ful stre3t, þat stek on his sides,
> A meré mantile abof, mensked withinne
> With pelure pured apert, þe pane ful clene
> With blyþe blaunner . . .   (ll. 152–55)

> *A neatly cut coat clung close to his flanks.*
> *His magnificent mantle was marvelously lined*
> *With furs trimmed to fit so the facings were seen.*
> *Fine ermine they were . . .*

Strayte, cote, meré, mantile, pelure, pured, pane, blaunner—all these fashion terms are French, and so are the courtly attitudes that Arthur's retainers resume as they try to come to terms with the Green Knight. I hope the translation preserves the contrast. A bit later, the same process—wide-eyed shock and unvarnished language giving way to courtly accommodation and French diction—plays itself out in the poem's account of the knight's axe.

In other words, the *Gawain*-poet is everywhere acutely sensitive to word choice, and a good translator must scramble to keep up with him. Like Chaucer, he uses subtle changes in language and register to reinforce his narrative. Recounting what goes on inside castle or court, he veers toward French diction, reinforcing the inside/outside dichotomy that runs throughout the poem. On those occasions I tried to follow him. Here Bertilak's lady is flattering Gawain in his bedroom:

> For þe costes þat I haf knowen vpon þe, kny3t, here,
> Of bewté and debonerté and blyþe semblaunt,

And þat I haf er herkkened and halde hit here trwee,
Þer shulde no freke vpon folde bifore yow be chosen.
(ll. 1272–75)

My version is correspondingly polysyllabic and I hope just as fulsome:

For the worth that I've witnessed, Gawain, in yourself,
Of beauty and breeding and brightness of semblance,
And all that I've heard of you, and hold for the truth,
There's no manner of man who could move me but you.

But the poet is equally at home with the rousing language of knightly adventure, describing, for example, how Arthur will not eat until he has heard of a marvel or until

. . . sum segg hym biso3t of sum siker kny3t
To joyne wyth hym in iustyng, in jopardé to lay,
Lede, lif for lyf, leue vchon oþer,
As fortune wolde fulsun hom, þe fayrer to haue. (ll. 96–99)

. . . someone came seeking a strong, proven knight
To join him in jousting for jeopardy's sake,
To lay life for life, and each freely allow
Fortune to favor him and foster his luck.

And, of course, he is supremely effective combining native and northern terms to describe the effects of cold weather:

Ner slayn wyth þe slete he sleped in his yrnes
Mo ny3tes þen innoghe in naked rokkez,
Þer as claterande fro þe crest þe colde borne rennez,
And henged he3e ouer his hede in hard iisse-ikkles.
(ll. 729–32)

Near slain with the sleet, the man slept in his irons
More nights than enough amid naked rocks
Where cold currents clattered and crashed from the crest
And hung in hard icicles over his head.

Every word that goes into his frequent depictions of fine clothes and sumptuous armor is telling. When Gawain is dressing to begin his journey to the Green Chapel, servants lay

> . . . a tulé tapit ty3t ouer þe flet,
> And miche watz þe gyld gere þat glent þeralofte;
> Þe stif mon steppez þeron, and þe stel hondelez,
> Dubbed in a dublet of a dere tars,
> And syþen a crafty capados, closed aloft
> Þat wyth a bry3t blaunner was bounden withinne. (ll. 568–73)

> *. . . a costly silk carpet to cover the floor,*
> *Where the gilded gear glittered and gleamed high aloft.*
> *He steps to the arms-stack and strokes the bright steel,*
> *Dressed in a doublet of Tharsian silk*
> *And a well-crafted cape that closed at the neck,*
> *With a lining of ermine eased into its length.*

But these are special cases. In the poem's finest passages language dissolves into a luminous transparency. Here, for example, a whole range of effects comes into play—the cyclical return of New Year's, the iron necessities of time, the poet's atypical concern for beasts and naked wretches, his feel for cold and snow, his wide-angle vision, and his favorite contrast between inside and outside—but none of them calls attention to itself. Instead, we seem to be looking directly through the poetry at the reality it represents, as if we were living it ourselves. Only a handful of poems in any language appeal to us so powerfully. This one often does. Here and elsewhere I hope I have done it some justice.

> Now ne3ez þe Nw 3ere, and þe ny3t passez,
> Þe day dryuez to þe derk, as Dry3tyn biddez;
> Bot wylde wederez of þe worlde waakned þeroute,
> Clowdes kesten kenly þe colde to þe erþe,
> Wyth ny3e innoghe of þe norþe, þe naked to tene;
> Þe snawe snitered ful snart, þat snayped þe wylde;
> Þe werbelande wynde wapped fro þe hy3e,

And drof vche dale ful of dryftes ful grete.
Þe leude lystened ful wel þat leȝ in his bedde,
Þaȝ he lowkez his liddez, ful lyttel he slepes (ll. 1998–2007)

Now the New Year draws nigh as night fades away.
Day drives off the dark as Destiny bids,
But wild, wintry weather awakened outside:
Clouds cast the keen, crackling cold to the earth
With North Wind enough to numb naked wretches.
Snow sleeted aslant, stinging wild beasts.
The weltering wind whipped the world from on high,
Driving each dale full of drift-piles of snow.
Gawain listened well, awake in his bed,
Though his eyelids are locked, full little he sleeps

The Text

Like the Old English epic *Beowulf, Sir Gawain and the Green Knight* came down to us in a single handwritten copy, bound in a small volume with three religious poems—*Pearl, Cleanness,* and *Patience*—commonly attributed to the same writer. In fact, *Gawain* and *Beowulf* have generally journeyed side by side. Both were part of a collection of old manuscripts assembled by Sir Robert Cotton (1571–1631) largely from works seized by Henry VIII in the dissolution of England's monasteries. In 1731 a fire destroyed two hundred of Cotton's books, which by then had been given to the kingdom. Although the *Gawain* volume came through largely unscathed, *Beowulf* was badly singed. Luckily, both poems were saved, and now their manuscripts can be seen in the same display case in the public gallery of the British Library, a gathering of England's greatest literary treasures. Not far away are Jane Austen's writing desk and Paul McCartney's scribbled lyrics to the song "Help."

The manuscript itself measures about seven by five inches, about the height of a modern paperback but a little broader and squarer. Twelve rough illustrations accompany the poems, including four full-page, but now rather faint pictures related to *Gawain*. The mere existence of these illustrations shows that someone thought enough of the poet's work to commission them.

The poem itself was written out in 101 stanzas, probably by a monk or professional scribe, in what was once a clear, workmanlike hand, now much decayed and frequently hard to make out. It is untitled but starts with a handsome capital *S* (for *Sipen*), whose earnestly decorated tail runs down the left margin to the bottom of the page. (See the facsimile on the following page.) The parts of the poem are not numbered in the manuscript, nor are they referred to there as *fits,* or *fitts* as modern editions often label them. That Chaucerian term was introduced when the work was first printed in the nineteenth century. The poem's four major divisions are shown by large, elaborate capital letters reinforced with a horizontal flourish that extends across the page to mark the second, third, and fourth parts. Smaller initial capitals without horizontals occur at the beginning of the description of Gawain's shield (l. 619), his first glimpse of Bertilak's castle (l. 763), the boar hunt (l. 1421), the second part of the fox hunt (l. 1893), and the Green Knight's return blows (l. 2259).

The standard modern edition of the text remains J. R. R. Tolkien and E. V. Gordon's 1925 work as revised for Oxford University Press by Norman Davis in 1967, with further corrections in 1972. This is the text I used for my translation.

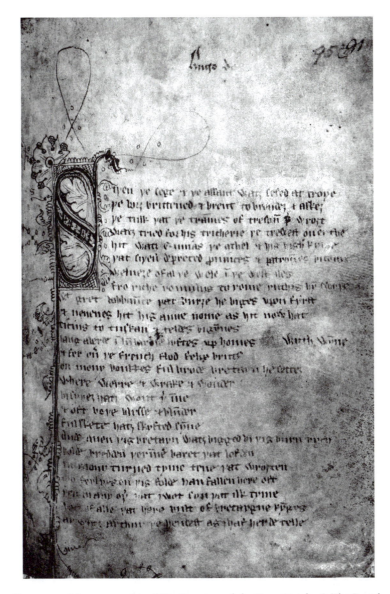

First page of the manuscript of *Sir Gawain and the Green Knight*. © The British Library Board. All rights reserved. British Library, Cotton Nero A.x., art 3, f.95.

Sample Lines in the
Original Middle English

Middle English is difficult and often creatively spelled, but some equivalencies are fairly regular. The character thorn (þ) would be written as *th* in Modern English. Yough or yok (ȝ) stands for *gh* here, although on occasion it can also signify the consonant *y*—as in *yikes* —or *z*. *U* and *v* are used interchangeably, as are *y* and *i*; our *wh* is written *qu*, as in *quen* (equals *when*). *Z* is often used at the ends of words where we would put *s* (*watz* equals *was*). The poet's accent system is much closer to ours. In these opening lines of Part 1, try pronouncing the verses. You should find four accents per line, except in the rhyming bob and wheel.

Siþen þe sege and þe assaut watz sesed at Troye,
Þe borȝ brittened and brent to brondez and askez,
Þe tulk þat þe trammes of tresoun þer wroȝt   *tulk: man*
Watz tried for his tricherie, þe trewest on erthe:
Hit watz Ennias þe athel, and his highe kynde,   *athel: noble*
Þat siþen depreced prouinces, and patrounes bicome   *depreced: conquered*
Welneȝe of al þe wele in þe west iles.   *wele: wealth*
Fro riche Romulus to Rome ricchis hym swyþe,   *swyþe: swiftly*
With gret bobbaunce þat burȝe he biges vpon fyrst,   *bobbaunce: pomp*
And neuenes hit his aune nome, as hit now hat;   *neuenes: names*
Tirius to Tuskan and teldes bigynnes,   *teldes: houses*
Langaberde in Lumbardie lyftes vp homes,
And fer ouer þe French flod Felix Brutus
On mony bonkkes ful brode Bretayn he settez
         wyth wynne,   *wynne: joy*
    Where werre and wrake and wonder
    Bi syþez hatz wont þerinne,   *wont: dwelled*

And oft boþe blysse and blunder
Ful skete hatz skyfted synne.   *skete, skyfted: quickly, shifted*

Ande quen þis Bretayn watz bigged bi þis burn rych,
Bolde bredden þerinne, baret þat lofden,   *Bolde, baret: bold [men], battle*
In mony turned tyme tene þat wroȝten.   *tene: trouble*
Mo ferlyes on þis folde han fallen here oft   *ferlyes: marvels*
Þen in any oþer þat I wot, syn þat ilk tyme.
Bot of alle þat here bult, of Bretaygne kynges,
Ay watz Arthur þe hendest, as I haf herde telle.   *hendest: most courtly*
Forþi an aunter in erde I attle to schawe,   *aunter, attle: adventure, intend*
Þat a selly in siȝt summe men hit holden,   *selly: wonder*
And an outtrage awenture of Arthurez wonderez.   *outtrage: most strange*
If ȝe wyl lysten þis laye bot on littel quile,
I schal telle hit as-tit, as I in toun herde,   *as-tit: directly*
      with tonge.
   As hit is stad and stoken   *stad, stoken: presented, set down*
   In stori stif and stronge,
   With lel letteres loken,   *lel, loken: faithful, locked*
   In londe so hatz ben longe.[1]   *In londe: in [our] land*

---

1. Some controversy surrounds this line. It could mean that the story has been known a long time or that it is written in the alliterative style (*letteres loken*) that has been common in England a long time.

Sir Gawain and the Green Knight

Part 1

ONCE the siege and the assault was ceased at Troy,[1]
The city battered and burnt down to brands and ashes,
The man who entangled that town in his treason
Was impeached for his perfidy, the purest on earth.
It was Aeneas the noble and his renowned kin,   5
Who put down whole provinces to make themselves princes
Of well nigh all wealth in the isles of the West.[2]
Rich, royal Romulus rushes toward Rome
And splendidly settles himself there in state
And names it with his name, the name it still bears.   10
In Tuscany Ticius[3] tosses up towers,
And in Lombardy Langobard lays out new homes.
Beyond the French Flood,[4] the lord Felix Brutus
Sets our brave Britain on hills and broad banks,
         full gay.   15
    Where war and wrack and wonder
    By turns have each held sway,
    And bouts of bliss and blunder
    Shift quickly to this day.

Now, since Britain was built by this baron, Lord Brutus,   20
Brash lads have bred there, bold lovers of battle.
In days that dawned after, they dealt out great dole

---

1. It was a traditional belief in England that Britain was established some time after the fall of Troy by Brutus, a grandson of Aeneas, the founder of Rome. The references to treason are unclear: the legendary Trojan traitor was Antenor, but some medieval stories also linked Aeneas to Troy's fall.

2. Western Europe.

3. An unknown figure.

4. The English Channel.

Amid portents and prodigies, piled high in this land
Beyond any I've heard of since those olden times.
But of all those brave builders, Britain's bold kings,   25
King Arthur stood highest, as I've heard it said.
And so I've resolved to tell you a story
That men have held one of the oddest on earth,
A marvel unmatched among all Arthur's wonders.
My lords, if you'll hark to this lay[5] but a little,   30
I shall tell it straight through as I heard it myself
                    once told.[6]
          The tale is written down,
          In verses stout and bold,
          With letters linked and bound,   35
          Like English poems of old.

This king lay at Camelot[7] one Christmas, they say,
With his levy of liegemen—a league of fine knights
Enrolled in the Round Table,[8] and rightfully so—
With carefree carousing and unexcelled mirth.   40
The lusty lords tilted in many a tourney.
Gentle knights jousted with joy and rare skill,
And then crowded the court for carol-dancing[9] and games,
For they held the feast there for fifteen full days[10]
With all meats and all mirth that a man could describe.   45
Such glamour and gleefulness! So glorious to hear!

---

5. The poet's term. A short narrative with marvelous happenings.

6. The writer's claim to have heard the story himself may not be true. No one has found an English source for it, but medieval audiences preferred traditional tales to newly made-up stories.

7. Arthur's chief stronghold.

8. The poet seems to have thought of "The Round Table" as simply a name for Arthur's court. When we later see court feasting, the knights sit at a high table and numerous sideboards (ll. 108–15), not at a round table.

9. In the late Middle Ages carols were dances. Participants often sang while dancing in a ring, giving rise to the modern meaning of the word.

10. Longer than the usual "Twelve Days of Christmas," which ran from December 25 to January 6, the Feast of the Epiphany.

Dear discourse by day and gay dancing at night,
The height of all happiness in halls and in chambers.
These lords and their ladies had little to wish for,
For the wealth of the world awaited them there: 50
The most notable knights beneath Christ Himself,
With the loveliest ladies that ever held life,
And the comeliest king to command their rich court;
For all these fair folk were in their fresh youth
                              combined.   55
  The luckiest on land,
  Their king the highest kind,
  A finer, choicer band
  Could hardly come to mind.

When the old year was dead, the first day of the new,[11]   60
Doubled-up dishes were served on the dais
When the king and his company came in the hall.
The chants in the chapel soon ceased to resound,
And calls clattered up from the clerks there and others:
"Noel!" they cried noisily, and "Noel!" again.   65
Then the rich folk ringed round to ready their gifts,
Praised their own presents and passed them by hand.[12]
They chattered and chaffered while choosing their bargains,
Ladies laughed loud although kisses were lost,
And you know those who won were not angry at all!   70
All this mirth made the many until time for their meat.
Then they washed themselves worthily and went to their places.
The first lords sat foremost, as befitted them best,
With glad Guenevere[13] glowing gay in their midst,
Adorning a dais well draped about   75
With shimmering silks and a ceiling above her

---

11. The English year of the time began on March 25, the Feast of the Assumption, but people also celebrated January 1, New Year's Day in the Roman tradition.

12. It sounds as though people in the court somehow bartered or auctioned off their gifts. Kissing seems to have come into it at some point, although no one is sure of the details.

13. Arthur's queen.

Of Tharsian[14] tapestries and stuff of Toulouse[15]
Embellished and bordered with bright, gleaming gems,
The most princely and precious that pennies might buy
        that day.   80
    The comeliest to see[16]
    Glanced round with eyes of gray.
    That he knew one fair as she,
    No honest man could say.

Yet King Arthur abstained while the others were served.   85
He was merry of mood and what's more a bit childlike.
He liked his life light and never did love
To lie long asleep, much less to sit still—
His bold blood buzzed so, and his busy, wild brain—
And he'd put himself under a proud, playful pledge   90
That he held to for honor. He never would eat
On such a high feast day until someone should tell him
Of a fabulous feat, unfolding a tale
Of some mighty marvel that he might believe
Of princes, of arms, or of other adventures;   95
Or till someone came seeking a strong, proven knight
To join him in jousting for jeopardy's sake,
To lay life for life, and each freely allow
Fortune to favor him and foster his luck.
Such was the king's wont when keeping his court   100
On any high feast day amid his fair folk
        in hall.
    And so with noble cheer,
    He stands apart and tall,
    Right glad to start the year   105
    Rejoicing with them all.

---

14. From Tharsia, a legendary kingdom east of Turkey.

15. French city on a Roman site near the Pyrenees.

16. Guenevere. It is left unclear, perhaps on purpose, whether she is being compared to other ladies or to the princely jewels above. Gray eyes are a standard feature of romance heroines.

Thus the strong king stood full straight by himself
In trifling talk with his friends at high table,
Where the good Sir Gawain[17] was seated by Guenevere
With Agravain Hard Hand[18] at his other side,   110
Sister's-sons to the king and staunch lords themselves.[19]
Above, Bishop Bawdwyn[20] began the high board,
With Yvain,[21] Urien's[22] son, sitting beside him.
These headed the hall and were handsomely served,
While scores of loyal knights sat round at the sideboards.   115
A clangor of trumpets proclaimed the first course—
Horns hung with bright banners that billowed beneath them—
Then a proud din of drums and piercing, sweet pipes
In wild, thrilling warbles, awoke hearts in the hall
And set them on high with their soul-swelling sounds.   120
Dainty dishes came dressed with the dearest of fare,
The finest and freshest, such a flood of new plates
The people were pressed to find space for them all,
Silver chargers filled full of fine dishes and stews
        set near.   125
   Each member of that crew,
   Feeds freely without fear.
   Twelve plates to every two,[23]
   Bright wine and foaming beer!

---

17. Although readers have disagreed about the pronunciation of *Gawain,* it seems clear when he rhymes it with *to frayne* (to pursue) (l. 489) or "how the fox watz slayn" (l. 1949) that the author was thinking Ga-WAYNE, with the accent on the second syllable.

18. Agravain de la Dure Main, one of Sir Gawain's brothers.

19. The seating arrangements are not overly clear, but Arthur's seat at the high table is probably vacant, with Guenevere on what would have been his left and Bishop Bawdwyn, the highest-ranking churchman present, on his right.

20. Bishop (of London?) and one of Arthur's early supporters according to the Middle English romance tradition.

21. A cousin of Gawain and Arthur.

22. King of Gore (a mythical British kingdom) and husband to Morgan le Fay.

23. Twelve dishes was a traditional number for a major feast. People were served in pairs and often shared the same plates as they ate.

Yet stop! I shall say nothing more of their service.   130
By now you must know that they wanted for naught,
But a new noise drew near them, a noise strange enough
To allow the king leave to raise food to his lips.[24]
For scarce had the minstrelsy ceased to resound,
And the first course of dinner been courteously served,   135
Than through the door hurtled a hair-raising stranger,[25]
The biggest and bulkiest man above ground.
From the neck to the waist he was well knit and wide,
And so lusty and long in his loins and his limbs,
He was halfway a giant on earth, by my head.   140
No burlier lord ever lived, I believe,
Yet a more graceful man of such might never rode.
Though his back and his breast—his whole body—seemed huge,
His waist and his stomach were worthily small,
And his face and his features befitted his form   145
            full clean.
        Yet they wondered at the hue
        Set in his countenance keen;
        He fared as bold knights do,
        But top to toe bright green!   150

Green was the man, and green all his gear:
A neatly cut coat clung close to his flanks.
His magnificent mantle was marvelously lined
With furs trimmed to fit so the facings were seen.
Fine ermine they were, as was the hood   155
That he loosed from his head and let hang from his shoulders.[26]
His handsome green hose gleamed as bright as his hood.
They cleaved to his calves, falling clean to his spurs,
Which blazed golden on bindings embellished with bars.

---

24. That is, odd enough to count as the marvel Arthur had been waiting for.

25. Later lines make it apparent that the Green Knight rides his horse into the hall where the court is feasting. That would be seen as a provocative, hostile act.

26. A fashionable arrangement.

He sat in soft stockings, like someone at peace,[27]   160
And each vestment he wore was the veriest green—
From the bands on his belt to the bright knots of gems
That were richly arranged in the lordly array
On his trappings and saddle, all stitched in fine silk.
It would try me to tell you the half of these trifles,   165
Embroidered about with gay birds and bugs.
All those gauds were in green, intertwined with fine gold.
The tabs of his horse-harness, breast band to crupper,
The enameled broad bosses adorning his bits,
The stirrups he stood in, were all the same color.   170
The bow of his saddle and its shimmering skirts
Glinted and glimmered with glowing green jewels.
The steed that he straddled shone green as the rest
                    beside.
        A green horse great and thick,   175
        No easy mount to ride,
        Yet in his bridle quick
        To answer to his guide.

What a grand sight that knight was, all garnished in green!
And the hair of his head was as green as his horse.   180
Fair, fanning tresses fell round his shoulders
While a beard like a bush bristled over his breast.
That heavy, broad beard and the green locks above it
Were clipped like a cape, elbow-length all around,
So the tops of his arms were hidden by hair—   185
Like a circular cope round the neck of a king.
His horse's thick mane almost matched the man's own,
Well combed out and crisped, and cunningly braided,
With glinting gold cords gleaming up through the green.
Through each hank of green wound another of gold.   190
Its dock and its forelock were decked out in like fashion.
Both were bound up with a glossy green band,

---

27. Medieval illustrations often show knights riding in long stockings out hunting or traveling, when no fighting was expected.

And its tail was entwined with twinkling, bright gems,
Trimly topped off with a tight-knotted thong
And polished gold bells that pealed as he moved.   195
No such horse on the earth, no such horseman, indeed,
Was ever beheld in that hall before then
                    with eye.
        His looks were lightning-bright,
        So said each one nearby.   200
        It seemed that no one might
        Withstand the strokes he'd ply.

Yet he had neither helm nor hard hauberk of mail,
Wore no breast piece of proof or plated steel arms,
No spear shaft or shield for smiting or thrusting,   205
But in one hand he held a twig of fresh holly,
That gleams at its greenest when groves are all bare,[28]
And in the other an axe, outlandish and huge,
A tough arm to tell of, try it who might.
Its massive, broad head measured more than a yard,   210
Its blade of green steel was garnished with gold.
The bit, burnished bright along its broad edge,
Was sharp as a razor and well shaped to shear.
He gripped the steel stoutly by a sturdy, broad shaft
Bound in black iron from bottom to top,   215
And engraved with bright green in a gracious design.
A lace lapped about it, locked close at the head.
It circled the shaft in loose swags and loops,
Tricked out with fine tassels attached close together,
Bound with bold buttons of brilliant, bright green.   220
The lord hove through the hall door and entered the room,
He drove to the dais, undaunted by danger.
Hailing no one at hand, he looked over their heads
And spoke his first sentence: "Where is," the man said,

---

28. This holly "bobbe," green in the depth of winter, is important to commentators who see the Green Knight as a vegetation figure. The man himself says only that it is a sign of peace (ll. 265–66); if so, it is oddly paired with the axe mentioned in the next line. The knight seems meant to be a confounding figure.

"The chief of this crew? It would please me to keep   225
That sire in my sight as I say what I've come
      to say."
He scanned the sitting rout—
Eyes roving every way—
As if he would make out   230
The one who held most sway.

They looked back at length, beholding this lord,
Each of them wondering what this could mean—
How that hulk and his horse could display such a hue,
As green as the grass, or yet greener it seemed,   235
Glowing brighter than rich green enamel on gold!
Engrossed with the sight of him, they gathered together,
Dumbfounded and doubtful of what he might do.
Those men had seen marvels, but none to match this.
Folk thought him a phantom or fairy indeed.   240
More than one noble was too numbed to answer.
Stunned by his speech, they sat stone-still and quiet.
A sudden dead stillness spread through the hall.
As if sunken in sleep, they slaked all their noise,
      struck shy.   245
   Not all, I think, in fright,
   Some courteously sat by—
   Let him who rules by right
   Deliver their reply.

King Arthur beheld him before the high dais,   250
And greeted him gaily, never aghast:
"Worthy knight," he said warmly, "I welcome you here.
I'm head of this hostel. Arthur I'm called.
Light lightly, my lord, and linger, I pray you,
Whatever you want here we'll weigh with you later."   255
"God save me, no!" the stranger knight answered.
"To tarry in talk is not my intent.
But as acclaim of you, lord, is lofted so loudly,
And your house and your heroes accounted the highest,
The strongest in steel-gear to go upon steeds,   260

The manliest men through the maze of the world—
As their triumphs in tourneys and battles attest—
And as courtesy counts for so much here, they claim,
Your fame and fair deeds drew me to your feast.
Know, noble lord, by this branch that I bear   265
That I pass here in peace, not pursuing hard strife.
Had I fared here in force and bent upon fighting,
I've a hauberk at home and a helmet to boot,
A shield and sharp spear of shining, bright steel,
And more weapons to wield, I know well, besides those.   270
But wishing no war, I came wearing soft garments.
Now, if you are as bold as it's bruited about,
You'll grant me, and goodly, the game that I ask,
         by right."
     King Arthur answered fair,   275
     And said, "Sir courteous knight,[29]
     If you crave battle bare,
     We'll find you one to fight."

"No, I fancy no fighting, in faith, as I told you,
These boys on your benches are beardless and weak.   280
If I were suited in steel on a high, haughty steed,
No man here could match me. None is mighty enough.
All I crave from this court is a gay Christmas game,
For it's Yuletide and New Year and brave youths abound here.
If one of your house holds himself truly hardy,   285
So brazen of blood and so bold in his brain,
That he dare strike a stroke and stand still for another,
I shall hand him my axe, this hard piece of war-work—
And right handsome its heft—to use as he will;
And I'll bide the first blow, as bare as I sit.   290
If some man is minded to try what I mean,
Let him come to me quickly and catch up this weapon.
I quitclaim it forever. He may hold it his own.
I'll suffer his stroke, lord, here on these stones
If you grant me your grace to give him another   295

---

29. Arthur's use of *courteous* here is probably ironic.

as I may;
And I'll offer him reprieve—
A twelvemonth and a day.[30]
Now quickly, by your leave,
Has any aught to say?"   300

If he stunned them at first, they now sat stiller yet,
The liegemen in hall, whether lofty or low.
Still sitting astride, he turned round in his saddle,
And direly rolled his red eyes left and right.
He bristled his brows, both the brightest of green,   305
And waved his big beard, baiting someone to rise.
When no one would speak, the knight snorted in scorn,
And shot back his shoulders, the better to shout.
"Is this Arthur's house?" he thundered at them.
"The retainers they talk of through regions and realms?   310
Where's your presumption, your pomp, and your pride?
Your gall and your grimness, your grudges and threats?
The rule and renown of the famous Round Table
Is now overwhelmed by one warrior's word—
All you drooping for dread and yet not a dint given!"   315
He laughed out so loud Arthur flushed in his grief:
Blood shot up for shame to shine in his cheeks
                    and face.
        His wrath rose like the wind
        And spread throughout the place.   320
        High-minded and thin-skinned,
        The king drew near apace

And said, "By my savior, your asking is foolish,
But such as you've sought, sir, it suits you to find.
No fighter here flinches for fear of your words.   325
Hand me that axe, and in high heaven's name,
I'll grant you the gift you've asked us to give you."
He leapt to him lightly and clasped the man's hand.
The other sprang eagerly off his great horse.

---

30. A traditional interval in romance as well as in legal agreements.

Now the king holds the axe and handles its haft, 330
Swipes with it swiftly, as if he would strike.
The fearsome green fellow towered before him,
The highest in the hall, and by more than a head.
With a stern look about he stroked his broad beard,
Then drew down his coat without care or concern, 335
No more doubtful or daunted by Arthur's sharp dints
Than if some man at the bench had brought him a bumper
of wine.
    Gawain sat by the queen.
    To Arthur he inclined 340
    And said with placid mien,
    "Sir,—let this fray be mine."

"Would you, worthy lord," Gawain said to the king,
"Bid me abandon this board and approach,
So that, sir, without shame I might stir from this table, 345
(That is, if my liege lady allows me to leave),
I would come to your counsel before your royal court.
For I consider it unseemly, as all men must see,
When an over-bold boast is blown high in your hall,
That you answer yourself, although surely you wish to, 350
While so many bold men sit about on these benches,
No men higher of will under heaven, I hope,
Nor better of body where battle is reared.
I'm your unworthiest warrior and feeblest of wit,
And losing my life would hurt least, lord, in truth.[31] 355
Having you for my uncle is my only merit.
Nothing blessed but your blood do I know in my body.
As this affair is so foolish and hardly befits you,
And as I asked first, sire, assign it to me.
If my claim is uncomely, your court may declare it 360
    without blame."
    Men's whispers buzzed the hall.

---

31. Gawain's speech is as elaborately polite as the Green Knight's is rude. It is also manifestly insincere. No one who hears him could think Gawain actually considers himself Arthur's unworthiest warrior.

The knights all said the same:
"Free Arthur from this brawl,
And give Gawain the game!"   365

The king commanded the knight to come down
And he rapidly rose and reached his lord's side,
Knelt in his honor and took hold of the axe.
Arthur let it go lightly and lifted his hand,
Gave Gawain his God's blessing and then gladly bidding   370
That his heart and his hand should be hardy, he said,
"Now be careful, my kinsman, to clout a stiff blow.
If you rap the man rightly, I reason, and truly,
You can bear any buffet that he may strike back!"
The axe in his hand, Gawain nears the huge warrior,   375
Who boldly abides there, nothing abashed.
He calls to Gawain, that giant in green,
"Let's repeat what we've plighted before we proceed.
But first I would know, knight, by what name you're called.
Tell me in truth and in terms I can trust."   380
"On my word," said the other, "Gawain is my name,
Who offers this dint, whatever comes after.
Twelve months from this morning you may mete me one back
With what weapon you will, though I'd withstand any other
                on earth."   385
        The giant warrior spoke:
        "Gawain! Sir, by my birth,
        I'm pleased to take this stroke
        From one of such high worth!"

"Begog!"[32] said the Green Knight, "Sir Gawain, I am glad   390
I shall find at your fist the favor I've asked for.
And you've rightly rehearsed, in the readiest words,
The scope of my covenant here with the king,
Save that you must assure me, good sir, by your truth,
That you'll seek me yourself, where so you may guess   395

---

32. Euphemism for "by God."

I may be found on the earth, to yield you such earnings
As you accord me in this courteous court."
"But where?" asked Gawain. "Where do you lodge?
I don't know your dwelling, by Him I hold dearest.
Nor do I know you, knight—your name or your court.   400
State both of these truly; tell me your title,
And I'll wear out my wits to wend there that day;
I swear to it, sir, by the truth of my soul."
"That's enough for this New Year. You needn't say more,"
Said the warrior in green to good Sir Gawain.   405
"If I'm telling the truth, when I've taken your tap,
And you've smitten me smartly, . . . well, then I shall speak
Of my house and my home and my name, as you ask.
Then come see how I serve you to settle our treaty.
If I speak no such speech, why, you speed all the better.   410
You may idle at home and hunt me no further.
　　　　Enough!
　　　Now take up your grim treasure.
　　　Let's see you deal a cuff."
　　　Gawain replies, "With pleasure!"   415
　　　And gives the blade a buff.

The Green Knight on the ground girds himself promptly;
He bows down a bit to bare his green nape.
His long, lovely locks he laid over his crown,
Let his shining skin show as the process required.   420
Gawain gripped the axe and heaved it up high,
Let his left foot advance a little before him,
And then brought it down neatly upon the knight's neck.
The axe's steel edge hurtled hard through the bones,
The skin and soft flesh were split sharply in two,   425
And the burnished steel blade bit into the ground.
The head from the neck toppled hard to the earth,
Where folk fended it from them as it tumbled forth.
Blood burst from the body, bright red on the green,
But the knight never faltered nor fell for all that.   430
He stoutly stepped forward upon his stiff shanks,
And roughly reached in through the ranks of the knights,

Laid hands on his head and held it up high.
Then he strides to his steed and snatches its reins,
Steps up in the stirrup and swings into the saddle.   435
His head he now holds in his hand by its hair,
And he steadily sat there astride his green steed,
Nothing dismayed, although now he was missing
            his head!
      He twisted left and right.   440
      His gruesome body bled.
      And many there took fright
      On hearing what he said.

For the head in his hand he holds high in the air.
To the dearest on the dais[33] he addresses the face,   445
Which lifted its eyelids and looked far and wide,
And its mouth said as much as you hear now from me:
"Look, Gawain, that you promptly depart as you pledged,
And ask loyally, lord, till you find me at last.
You swore that you would, as these worthies can witness.   450
Seek the Green Chapel, I say, to receive
Such a dint as you've dealt me, to match your deserts.
I'll knout you a fine knock next New Year's morn.
I'm the Green Chapel Knight, and not a few know me.
If you fare forth to find me, and ask, you won't fail.   455
So come, or a craven be called—and correctly."
With a rampageous jerk, he wrenched round his reins
And hurled out of the hall, his head in his hand,
So that fire from the flints flashed behind the steel hooves.
Where he went next not one of them knew,   460
Just as none could declare what country he came from.
            What then?
      Though Gawain and Arthur now
      May laugh and smile again,
      He was, as all avow,   465
      A marvel among men.

---

33. This may be Guenevere, whom the Green Knight supposedly means to
frighten.

Although King Arthur wondered at heart,
He let no sign be seen but said with high spirits
To his courteous queen in the speech of the court:
"Dear dame, never let this day's doings dismay you.   470
Such craft well becomes a Christmastide feast,
As do skylarking, interludes,[34] laughter, and songs,
Or dalliance and dancing of damsels and knights.
Nonetheless, to my meat I may set me at last,
For I've witnessed a wonder. I won't deny that."   475
He glanced at Gawain and gaily he said,
"Now hang up your axe.[35] It has hewn enough here."
It was done up over the dais to hang from the drapes,
A marvel to men who minded to look,
And a sign all could see that their stories were true.   480
Then they turned to the table, those two friends together,
Sir Gawain and his Sire, and were suitably served
With double-sized dainties befitting their dignity,
And all manner of meats, and with minstrelsy too.
Thus they idled at ease till the day fitly ended   485
            in cheer.
      Now think you well, Gawain:
      You mustn't shrink with fear,
      The adventure to attain,
      You've undertaken here.   490

---

34. Short dramatic pieces sometimes staged during banquets.
35. Idiom for "Stop what you're doing." Arthur means it literally as well as figuratively.

PART 2

THIS green man was Arthur's first gift of the season—
The young, coming year—just the challenge he yearned for.
Although little was said as they sat at their supper,
A hard work's ahead of them; their hands are crammed full.
Gawain was glad to begin that strange game.   495
But if it ends heavily, hold it no wonder;
For though drinking may make a man merry in mind,
A year slides by swiftly, never the same,
And the early days seldom accord with the end.
Yuletide soon yielded to the rest of the year,   500
The sequence of seasons ensuing by turns.
Christmas must cede to cold comfort in Lent.[36]
Lent flays our flesh with fish and plain fare.
But then the world-weather quarrels with winter.
Cold unclasps its clamps as the clouds lift on high.   505
The fair rain falls rustling in fruitful warm showers,
Plying soft plains. Flowers appear.
Green ground and grove go gowned in new verdure.
Busy birds build and bravely sing out
For soft summer's solace that settles thereafter   510
                    on hills.
        And blossoms swell and blow
        By rich hedgerows and rills,
        And notes the wild birds know
        Fill woods with pleasant trills.   515

Then summer itself arrives with soft winds,
When Zephyrus[37] breathes on the seeds and young shoots.

---

36. The forty-day period of fasting leading up to Easter.
37. The west wind. Associated with spring.

How glad is the green herb that grows from them then,
As the dampening dew drips from its leaves,
To bide there in bliss for bright beams from the sun!   520
But harvest comes hastening and hails him[38] full quickly,
Warns him for winter to wax and grow ripe,
And drives in the drought so that dust rises up
From the face of the fields, flying high in the air.
In the sky the wild winds wrestle the sun.   525
Leaves drop from the linden and light on the ground,
The grass turns to gray that was green at first,
And all ripens and rots that had risen in spring.
And so the year turns, on yesterdays many.
Winter waxes again as the world says it must,   530
        no jest.
    Till Michaelmas's moon[39]
    Shone down, in winter dressed.
    Then thinks Gawain full soon
    Of his unquiet quest.   535

Yet till All Hallows' Day[40] he houses with Arthur,
Who furnished a feast there to honor his friend,
With bliss and abundance about the Round Table.
The courteous knights and comely, fine ladies
Grieved for Gawain, for they loved the good lord;   540
Still they went through the motions that men do in mirth—
Gentles, though joyless, made jokes for his sake.
And yet, sad after supper, he speaks to his uncle
Of the trail he must tread, and talks to him plainly:
"Now, lord of my life, I must leave, if I may.   545
You know the terms of the task I took on,
To weigh its ills further would waste more good words.
I must seek out that stroke, and start, sir, tomorrow.
I'll find that green fellow if faith will but guide me."

---

38. The green herb, that is.
39. September 29, the feast of Saint Michael the Archangel.
40. November 1, All Saints' Day.

Then the noblest knights came in numbers together: 550
Yvain and Eric and others full many,
Sir Dodinal the Wild, the bold Duke of Clarence,
Lancelot, Lionel, Lucan the good,
Sir Bors and Sir Bedivere, both brawny knights,
And more mighty men, like Mador de la Porte.[41]   555
All this courteous company comes to the king
To counsel the knight with keen care in their hearts.
A soft swell of sadness swept through the hall
That worthy Gawain should wend on that errand,
To suffer a stroke and not strike back another.   560
    Stern test.
  The knight himself seemed glad,
  Said, "What? Forsake my quest?
  In destinies good or bad
  We men must do our best."   565

He dwells there that day and dresses the next,
Asks early for armor, sees all of it brought.
First a costly silk carpet to cover the floor,
Where the gilded gear glittered and gleamed high aloft.
He steps to the arms-stack and strokes the bright steel, 570
Dressed in a doublet of Tharsian silk
And a well-crafted cape that closed at the neck,
With a lining of ermine eased into its length.
They set on steel shoes[42] to shield the man's feet,
His lower legs lapped in lovely steel greaves,   575
Knee pieces knotted on, polished and neat,
Their caps fastened firmly with fine golden fittings.
Bright cuisses[43] next that completely enclosed
His thick, brawny thighs, attached with stout thongs,
Then the rustling rings of his rugged mail corselet   580

---

41. All are knights associated with King Arthur in French romances.
42. Sabots, the martial steel footgear the Green Knight was not wearing in Part 1, line 160. Greaves are armor to cover a warrior's shins.
43. Thigh armor.

Covered him close over sumptuous cloth.
Well-burnished braces upon both his arms,
Gay elbow pieces, gloves of steel plate,
And a wealth of good gear that would work to his gain,
   well plied.   585
  His coat of arms displayed,
  Spurs buckled on with pride,
  He bore a sword well made,
  With silk fixed to his side.

When he was hasped in his armor, his harness was rich, 590
Its least latchet or loop illumined with gold.
Armed for war as he was he went off to Mass,
Honored and offered to Christ at the altar.
Then he comes to the king and his company in court,
Takes his leave most politely of ladies and lords, 595
Who kissed and commended him kindly to Christ.
They girt Gringolet[44] with a gaily decked saddle
That gleamed with the glitter of many gold fringes,
New nailed with bright nails for the knight's present need.
The bridle was bound and bespangled with gold. 600
Breast straps and saddle skirts suitably shone;
The crupper and caparison accord with the saddle bows,
All arrayed in bold red and enriched with gold studs
That glinted and gleamed like the glance of the sun.
He holds up the helm and hastily kisses it— 605
It was strengthened full stoutly and well stuffed inside.
It sat high on his head, hasped at the back,
With a costly band clasped to a cleat by the neck guard,
Embroidered and bound with the brightest of gems
On broad bands of silk with brave birds on each border, 610
Such as pictures of parrots preening between
Turtles and trueloves[45] as thickly entangled,
As if women had worked on them seven full winters,

---

44. Gawain's horse.
45. Turtledoves and love knots, appropriate decorations for a lover.

well sped.
A crown more costly yet,   615
Encircled his fair head,
Of diamonds closely set
On flashing gold and red.

When they showed him his shield of shimmering scarlet
Adorned with a pentangle painted in gold,   620
He seized its strong strap to sling round his neck.
The shield suited the hero, beseeming him well.
How its pentangle pictured his perfect nobility,
I intend now to tell, though it hold up my tale.
It was a symbol King Solomon[46] set for his people   625
To betoken pure truth, and truly it does,
For the figure runs freely to five separate points,
And each line overlaps and is latched to another,
So not one ever ends, and Englishmen call it,
Far and near, as I'm told, by the name "endless knot."[47] 630
This figure befitted Gawain's fulgent arms,
For faithful in five things, and five ways in each,
That peer was well proved, like gold purified,
Void of all villainy, with virtues adorned,
                in town.   635
    The pentangle painted new
    He wore on shield and gown—
    A man whose words were true;
    No finer could be found.

For first he was faultless in his five senses,[48]   640
And never had failed in all his five fingers,

---

46. Biblical king known for his wisdom.

47. There is no evidence that England made much of the pentangle, an old magic and mystical Christian symbol apparently not associated with Gawain until the author made the connection here. His is the first recorded use of the term *pentangle* in English.

48. Note that this stanza concerning the five fives has twenty-five long lines leading up to the "bob and wheel."

And his faith was well fixed on the five fatal wounds
That Christ caught on His cross, as our Creed clearly tells us.
And wherever the man was mixed in a melee,
He thought upon this above anything else: 645
His fortitude was founded upon the five joys
That heaven's queen held at the hands of her child.[49]
For this reason the hero had rightly arranged
That she should be shown inside his strong shield,
For beholding her image, his heart never failed. 650
The fifth five I find he held fast to were these:
Freedom and *friendship* before any others;
His *cleanness* and *courtesy* were certain and constant;
And his chief point was *pity.* These peerless five
Stood high in this hero above any other.[50] 655
All these five fives were fixed firm in the knight,
Each upholding the others so none ever ended,
And fastened on five points that never had failed.
Not one was the same, yet not sundered at all,
No end to it anywhere I ever found, 660
However you entered, wherever you left.
Thus that symbol was suitably set on his shield
In royal red gold against a red ground,
The pure and proud pentangle as people have named it
          with lore.[51] 665
    And that was his array,
    Except the lance he bore.
    He gave his friends good day—
    He feared for evermore.

---

49. Usually listed in the *Gawain*-poet's day as the Annunciation, the Nativity, the Resurrection, the Ascension, and Mary's Assumption. The five Joyful Mysteries of the Rosary are probably not meant here. They were not officially adopted until the sixteenth century.

50. The five fives are these: (1) Gawain's five senses (his moderation); (2) his five fingers (his actions); (3) the five wounds of Christ (feet, hands, and side); (4) the five joys of Mary; and (5) his own chief virtues—freedom (generosity), friendship, cleanness (chastity), courtesy, and pity (compassion)—a somewhat arbitrary assortment that the poet seems to have invented for use here.

51. That is, people of learning.

Setting spurs to his steed, he sprang forth on his way,   670
So that stone-fire sparked up from his strong horse's hooves.
The watchers were woeful and weakened at heart.
They said truly enough, every knight to the next,
In care for the comely one: "By Christ it's a shame
That you, lord, are lost, our most noble of life!   675
His equal on earth would be hard to discover.
It would have been better, a work of more wit,
To ordain him a duke, for that was his due.
To lead other lords of the land would beseem him—
Wiser in all ways than waste him for naught.   680
Lose his head to an elf! And only for pride!
How can a king take his counsel in court
From knights' feast-day fribbles and such foolish games?"
Many warm tears went to water their eyes
When the hero set out from Arthur's fine castle   685
                    that day.
          He lodged at no abodes,
          But bravely took his way
          Down many tangled roads,
          As I heard my author say.[52]   690

And so Gawain rides through the wide realm of Logres.[53]
In Holy God's name, though his errand was irksome.
Lingering alone, many nights he lies out
And feeds as he finds, not on fare that he favors.
No friend but his horse in the holts and the hills.   695
No guide but good God to give him his way,
Till he wandered full nigh to the north end of Wales.
The islands of Anglesey[54] he holds on his left
As he fares across fords in the forelands he passes.

---

52. Like many medieval authors, the poet hints at a source for his story. But he might not have had one.

53. Arthur's kingdom, from the Welsh word for England. The poet imagines it somewhere in the south of Britain.

54. Anglesey itself and nearby smaller islands in the Irish Sea off Wales.

He crosses at Holy Head,[55] then comes to the coast   700
And the wilds of the Wirral, where few ever were
Who had either God or each other at heart.[56]
And always he asked everyone that he passed
If they knew of a knight who went wholly in green
Or of any Green Chapel on grounds thereabout.   705
They answered with nays. Not one of them knew
Or had seen such a sight—a lord of such semblance,
          all green.
     The knight took unknown ways
     Through country poor and mean.   710
     He'll wander many days
     Before that chapel's seen.

He climbed many cliffs in coarse, broken country,
Far, far afield, the friendless one rides.
At each ford over floods that he faced as he went,   715
He found fierce foes to front him more often than not,
And so foul and such fell ones that fight them he must.
In those mountains the man met with so many marvels
It would tax me to tell the tenth part of the tale.
Sometimes he struggles with serpents and wolves,   720
Or rampaging trolls who roved the high rocks,
Or with bears or wild bulls, or bold, savage boars,
Or ogres that harried him from high on the fells.
Had he not been so doughty and devoted to God,
Doubtless the knight would have died, and full often.   725
Yet more bitter than battle was winter's sharp bite
When the shining cold rain poured in sheets from the clouds
And froze as it fell on the earth's pallid face.

---

55. Probably Holywell, where Saint Winifred was beheaded on the Dee Estuary, not modern Holy Head on Anglesey.

56. Gawain's route becomes clearer as he goes along. Leaving Camelot, he rides the length of the country to north Wales and then turns back toward England and the Wirral, a peninsula between the rivers Mersey and Dee, near present-day Liverpool.

Near slain with the sleet, the man slept in his irons
More nights than enough amid naked rocks   730
Where cold currents clattered and crashed from the crest
And hung in hard icicles over his head.
Thus in peril and pain from one plight to the next,
The knight crosses the country until Christmas Eve,[57]
        alone.   735
    Sir Gawain at that good tide
    To Mary made his moan,
    That she should be his guide
    To some shelter of his own.

By a mountain that morning he merrily rides   740
And enters a wilderness, wintry and wild.
High hills on each hand and a holt of trees under—
Huge hoary oaks, by the hundred together,
With low hazels and hawthorns disheveled and snarled,
And rough, ragged ravels of moss reaching down.   745
Many birds, but not blithe ones, sat on bare twigs,
Pitifully piping for pain of the cold.
The knight on his Gringolet travels beneath them;
Through marshes and mires the man rides alone,
Concerned for his soul, should he not find some chapel   750
To celebrate Christ, who on that chosen night
Was born of a maiden, our battles to quell.
And so the knight sighed as he said, "I beseech you,
Jesus and Mary, good mother so mild,
For some harbor at hand where I may hear Mass   755
And your matins tomorrow. Meekly I ask it,
And piously pray my Pater and Ave
        and Creed.[58]
    He rode along in prayer,
    Repenting each misdeed.   760

---

57. December 24, that is, the day of Christmas Eve.
58. Paternoster (Our Father); Ave Maria (Hail, Mary); and the Credo (The Apostles' Creed).

He crossed himself most fair,[59]
And called, "Now Christ me speed!"

No more had he crossed himself carefully thrice
Than he beheld in the woods a hall on a hill.
On a mound in a moat it mounted through boughs   765
Of towering trees overtopping its ditches:
The comeliest castle a knight could command,
Gleaming on grass in a goodly large park,
With a sharp-pointed palisade planted full thick,
To mark off the forest for more than two miles.   770
The knight stopped there, scanning his side of the castle
As it shimmered and shone through the sparkling oaks,
Then he hales off his helm and humbly gives thanks
To Jesus and Julian,[60] gentle souls both,
That kindly consented to come to his aid.   775
"Now award me," he said, "a good welcome as well!"
And he goads on good Gringolet with his gilt heels.
By chance he had come on the castle's main causeway,
And this brought him soon to the bulky, great bridge,
        unasked.   780
    The bridge was stoutly drawn.
    The gates were bolted fast.
    The walls looked down with scorn.
    They feared no winter's blast.

Gawain in his saddle sat still by the side   785
Of the dark double ditch defending the place.
The wall pierced the water, went wonderfully deep,
And towered above him at the top of its height.
Squarely hewn stone stretched aloft to the cornices,
With boldly hung battlements in the best style   790
And strong, sparkling turrets spaced in between,
With many a loophole latched and locked tight.

---

59. Made the sign of the cross.
60. Saint Julian, patron saint of hospitality.

He had never beheld a better built barbican,[61]
And he saw there behind it a hall of great height:
Tall, slender towers whose tops reared like antlers,   795
Sharp shining spires shooting straight to the sky,
With finely shaped finials fittingly made.
Square chalk-white chimneys were common enough there;
They shimmered and shone on high steeples and roofs.
Such painted gay pinnacles prinked up the place,   800
So many embrasures, and mounted so high,
It appeared like a castle pared out of paper.[62]
To the man on his mount it seemed a marvel indeed.
He cast in his mind for some means to get in,
To harbor there happily for Christ's holy feast,   805
      so bright.
   He called, and soon there came
   A porter most polite,
   Who gave his post and name
   And hailed the wandering knight.   810

"Good sir," said Gawain, "would you serve me and ask
The high lord of this house if he'll harbor a guest?"
The porter swore by Saint Peter,[63] saying, "Surely I think
He'll welcome you, lord, for as long as you like."
He stepped away shortly but soon he was back   815
With an assembly of servants to receive the good knight.
They dropped the great drawbridge and decently waited,
Then kneeled to the noble on the numbing cold ground
To welcome him well, in accord with his worth.
They called him across, cast open the gate,   820
And he bid them to rise and rode over the bridge.
Many men met him to help him dismount.
Servers came forward to stable his steed.

---

61. Defensive work, especially the gatehouse.
62. Paper castles, elaborately designed and ornamented in gold, were used as decorations at feasts.
63. Saint Peter, the porter at heaven's door.

Knights crowded near, newly come from the keep
And eager to usher him into the hall.   825
When he haled off his helm, they hastened together,
To set it aside and serve him with care.
His brand and bright shield were both borne away,
And he graciously greeted each one on the ground.
Many proud peers met the prince there to honor him,   830
As, still suited in steel, he strode into the hall.
A fair, well-laid fire flamed up fierce on the floor,
And the castle's high ruler arrives from his room
To nobly acknowledge his guest, the new knight.
"Welcome!" he wished him. "Wield all as you like.   835
What is here is your own, I surrender the house
            to you."
        "God thank you!" said Gawain,
        "May Christ reward you too."
        And then in joy the twain   840
        Embrace as such men do.

Gawain looked on the lord who lent him that greeting,
And thought he was mighty, the man who ruled there—
A princely great person in the prime of his life.
Broad was his beard, and as brown as a beaver,   845
Stiff in his stance on the strongest of shanks,
A face fierce as fire, and yet friendly in speech.
He seemed suited well to the state that he kept,
The master of men in that marvelous castle.
He escorted the knight to a chamber and called   850
For a suitable servant to see to his needs.
Many good servitors sprang to his summons,
Brought Gawain to a bower filled with beautiful bedding,
Costly silk curtains with clear golden hems,
And coverlets quilted with comely square panes—   855
Fur lined, embroidered, embellished full richly.
The drapes ran on ropes hung from rings of fine gold;
The wall-tapestries came from Toulouse and from Tharsia,
With the like laid as carpets the length of the floor.
They untied his war gear while talking of trifles,   860

Removing his mail and plate armor besides;
Then ready retainers brought him rich robes
To try on at will and wear if he would.
When he found one he favored and fastened it round him,
And it fell from his shoulders to full, flowing skirts,   865
The season of spring seemed to spread through the room—
Or so the knights said upon seeing those colors
Shining and shimmering on his stout limbs.
Christ never created a comelier knight,
                    they thought.   870
          However he came there,
          He seemed the best in aught—
          A prince without compare
          In fields were fierce men fought.

A chair by the chimney, where charcoal was burning,   875
Was drawn for the champion, well covered to cosset him
With cushions and quilts, full quaintly stitched.
They cloaked the good man in a marvelous mantle,
Of bright woven cloth, bravely embroidered
And well furred within with a wealth of fine pelts,   880
The best ermine on earth, and a hood of the same.
He sat on that settle in splendid estate
And warmed himself wisely, freed from his wants.
Fresh servants furnished a fair trestle table,
Clad in clean cloth that shone clear and white,   885
And set with a saltcellar and good silver spoons.
He washed as he would and then went to his meat.
The salvers they served him were seemly enough,
Big bowls of broth boiled with rich seasonings,
Double-filled as was fitting, and followed by fishes,[64]   890
Some baked in bread, some broiled on the coals,
Some seethed, some in stews with savory spices,
And well-seasoned sauces to suit every one.
Gawain called it a feast full freely and often.

---

64. It is still the day before Christmas, a fast day when no meat could be eaten.

They urged him to eat and cheerfully added,   895
      full fine:
  "Forgive this fast-day fare.
  Tomorrow you may dine."[65]
  Gawain made mirth to spare,
  His wit well warmed with wine.   900

Then questions were asked in most courteous fashion,[66]
Through polished enquiries posed to the prince,
Till he kindly acknowledged he came from the court
Where the renowned King Arthur so regally ruled—
The lofty, rich lord of the lustrous Round Table—   905
And the wanderer they'd welcomed was no less than Gawain,
Come there at Christmas, for such was his chance.
When the lord of the castle learned whom he kept
He laughed out aloud in delight at the news.
All the knights in that keep rejoiced and took care   910
To meet their new guest the first moment they might:
One whose pride and prowess and pureness of manners
Append to his person and always are praised.
His honor excels above all men's on earth.
Each noble who saw him said soft to his brother: 915
"Now sure we shall see true seemly behavior,
And crowning examples of courtly discourse.
How to speed in our speech we may learn without straining,
Since we host such a champion, a captain of courtesy.
God has given us grace, to be sure,   920
That He grants for our good such a guest as Gawain
When men blithe for His birth sit on benches in church
      and sing.
  The meaning of manners pure,
  This man shall surely bring.   925
  I warrant all who hear
  May talk love like a king!"

---

65. Tomorrow will be Christmas, when the fast is lifted.

66. Errant (wandering) knights in Arthurian stories often wanted to keep their
identities to themselves.

When the dinner was done and the dear man arose,
It had nearly grown dark and night was at hand.
Chaplains had chosen their way to their chapels   930
And rung men in rightly for readings and prayer,
Evensong service for that holy season.
The lord comes to listen, and his lady as well,
Although she sat apart in a private closed pew.
When Gawain at his gayest goes down to the chapel,   935
The lord catches his coat and calls him to sit;
He hails Gawain nobly and names the good knight
The goodliest guest he could greet in the world.
Gawain bade him thanks; they embraced like two brothers
And sat side by side till the service was ended.   940
Then it pleased the lord's lady to look on the knight.
She came from her closet with her comeliest maidens,
But she was the fairest of flesh and of face.
Her carriage and color eclipsed all the others:
She was gayer than Guenevere, Gawain had to grant.   945
She courteously crossed through the chancel to meet him
With a lady to lead her, clasping her hand—
One far older than she, an ancient it seemed,
But held in high honor by all those about.
The looks of those ladies were nothing alike.   950
For if one was unwilted, the other was withered.
Rose red was the one in her person and raiment;
Rough, wrinkled cheeks ruined the other one's face.
One wore a headdress bedecked with dear pearls,
And her breast and bright throat, both bare to the gaze,   955
Shone out more splendid than snow spread on hills.
Her friend wore a wimple wrapped round her waddles.
She clothed her black chin in cloth white as chalk,
And enfolded her forehead in furrows of silk,
Tricked out in turrets and trifling touches,   960
So that nothing was bared but her beetling brows.
Her eyes and her nose, and her loose, hanging lips—
All blubbered and bleary—were baleful to see.
A worshipful woman was this one indeed!
      Not so!   965

Beneath her bulky waist,
Her bulging buttocks show.
Much sweeter to the taste,
That one she had in tow.

Gawain gazed at the gay one, who glanced back at him.   970
With the sire's gracious leave, he stepped to their side.
The elder he hails with a humble, low bow;
But the more lovesome lady he laps in his arms,
And kisses her comely with courteous speech.
They crave his acquaintance, and quickly he offers   975
His service to both, supposing it suits them.
They take him between them and talking they lead him
To a fire-lighted alcove and call for spiced cakes.
These are speedily served, unsparingly too,
And good, winning wine to go with them as well.   980
The lighthearted lord leaped up full often
And moved them to mirth with many good jests.
He haled off his hood, hung it high on a spear,
And urged any who would to win it with worship
By making most mirth for that merry Yule season,   985
Saying, "I'll try, by my truth, to contend with the best,
With all my friends' help, ere I yield up my hood!"
Thus with pleasing palaver he lightens their minds,
To gladden Gawain with such games in the hall
                    that night   990
          Until it grew so late,
          The lord called out for light.
          Gawain took leave full straight,
          To sleep well, if he might.

On that morning when each man remembers the time   995
That Christ came to earth to be killed for our cause,
Goodwill wells up wide through the world for his sake.
And so did it there for that dear day's delights.
Both large meals and lesser came laudably cooked.
Good men dressed the dais with delicate fare.   1000
The ancient old lady sits highest of all,

With the lord, I believe, lodged by her side.
Gawain and the wife sit to one side together;
At the high table's center they're suitably served.
Then all through the hall as the household thought best   1005
Each man took his meal by his rank as he must.
Ah, what meat and what mirth and amusement they had!
It would trouble my wits to tell it, in truth,
No matter what toil I put into the telling.
Yet I believe that Gawain and the lord's noble lady   1010
Took such comfort in their company, cast there together,
Through their dainty, fine dalliance and undisclosed words
(Though fair ones and fitting and free from all harm),
That their playing surpassed the most princely of games
                    now known.   1015
      Drums, pipes, and horns by turns
      Rumble, screak, and moan.
      Each man minds his concerns,
      And those two mind their own.

They pleased themselves perfectly for two pleasant days   1020
And the third, as contenting, that followed thereafter.
The joy on Saint John's day was gentle to hear;
Then the feasting was finished for most of those folk.
The guests planned to go in the gray of the morning,
So they dabbled and dallied till long after dark,   1025
Drinking and dancing deep into the night.
At last, and full late, they left for their chambers.
Each taking his way as well as he could.
Gawain stood to leave, but the lord made him linger,
Bid him come to his chamber to sit by the chimney,   1030
And there he detained him to thank him full well
For the gracious regard the good knight had shown him,
To honor his house at the height of that season,
And accord his choice company to all in the castle,
Saying, "As long as I live, it enlarges my fame   1035
That Gawain was my guest at God's birthday feast."
"Ah," Gawain answered, "in good faith, it is yours—
All the honor is yours, sir; may heaven reward you!

I accept your commands and will cleave to your will.
I'm now bound to obey you in big things or small,   1040
          I say."
     Yet though the kind lord tries
     To make the good knight stay,
     Gawain has one reply:
     He must be on his way.   1045

Then his heedful host asked him what awful affair
Had made the good man at that most holy time
Quit his king's court and come out alone,
Before the high holidays even had ended.
"What you say," Gawain answered, "strikes straight to the truth: 1050
A hard errand hailed me from home, and in haste,
For I'm summoned to seek out an uncertain place,
And where in the world I must wend, I don't know;
Yet I'd not fail to find it before New Year's morn,
For all the land that's in Logres, so help me Our Lord.   1055
So, sir, I appeal—I implore you—speak plainly
And tell me now honestly if you ever heard
Of any Green Chapel, wherever it is,
And its guardian, a knight who goes all in green.
I offered my oath to a treaty between us   1060
To meet that green man there, and must if I live.
Now that the New Year is nearly upon us,
I would look on that lord if God will allow it,
More gladly, Christ knows, than gain any good else.
And so, if you will, I must wend on my way.   1065
I've hardly three days yet to honor my oath,
And I'd sooner be slain, lord, than swerve from my task."
Laughing, the lord said, "Then linger here longer!
You shall get to your goal before the time's gone—
The Green Chapel, that is—so grieve you no more.   1070
You shall loll here abed and lounge at your leisure,
Well after dawn and depart New Year's Day
For your meeting that morning and manage your quest
          right there.
     So stay till then, I say.   1075

Rest here. There's time to spare.
We'll set you on your way.
You've not two miles to fare."

Gawain grew full glad and gaily he laughed:
"Now I thank you for this above all other things.   1080
Since my chance is achieved, why, I choose as you will
To dwell here with you and do all you demand."
The sire seized Gawain and set him beside him,
Had the ladies brought in to enlarge their delight,
And with suitable pastimes they solaced themselves.   1085
The good lord waxed gallant, with gay, jesting words,
Spoke like one witless, till they watched him in wonder.
He called to the champion, crying aloud,
"You dared to assure me you'd do as I say.
Will you stand by that statement, sir, starting now?"   1090
"I intend to, in truth," said the knight, leaning toward him.
"While I board in this building, I'll obey your commands."
"As you labored, my friend, to fare here from afar
And have scarcely slept since, you've had less than your share
Of slumber or sustenance, I'm sure," said the lord.   1095
"So remain in your room, and rest at your ease
Tomorrow, till Mass-time, then go to your meat—
When you will—with my wife. She will wait on you, sir,
And accord you her company till I'm back in court.
                Stay here   1100
       While I see in the sun
       Out hunting far and near."
       Gawain replies, "Yea, done."
       And bows with courtly cheer.

"Yet more," said the man, "let us make an agreement: 1105
What I win in the wood, I'll grant you with goodwill,
And you just as gladly must give up your gains.
Say that you'll swap, sir. Swear to it now—
Whatever we win, be it worthless or worthy."
"By God," said Gawain, "I grant all you will.   1110
It's a joy to me, lord, to join in your games."

"A bumper!" the sire called. "Our bargain is sealed!"
He laughed with Gawain and the lighthearted ladies.
They drank as they chatted and chaffed without check,
These fine lords and ladies, as long as they pleased,   1115
And finally with speech in the fairest French fashion,
They stood talking softly, slow to take leave.
At last with fond kisses they catch up their cloaks.
Link boys then held lighted torches aloft
To conduct those companions to comfortable beds,   1120
        well made.
    But first the men recalled
    The spoils they meant to trade.
    The old lord of that hall
    Would see those debts were paid.   1125

PART 3

WELL before daybreak the fine folk rose up.
Guests who were going called out to their grooms,
Who hand forth their horses saddled and harnessed
And attend to their tackle and truss up their bags.
Rich lords well arrayed and ready to ride   1130
Swing up on their steeds and shorten the reins.
Each takes his way, wherever he wants.
The lord of the land was scarcely the last
To fit himself out to go forth with his fellows.
He ate a sop hastily once he'd heard Mass,   1135
And then bustles with bugle calls about in the fields.
By the time the first daylight fell on the folds,
Master and men were mounted on high.
The huntsmen hastened to couple their hounds.
They clanged open the kennels and called the dogs out,   1140
Hoisted their horns and blew three bold blasts.[67]

---

67. The three horn notes marshal the hunters and dogs. The deer hunt that fol-
lows is of the sort called "by bow and stable." The herd is located before the
hunt, possibly by a lymer, or scenting dog. The hunt itself uses pack hounds—
brachets (like modern harriers or foxhounds) to chase the game—and grey-
hounds (today's deerhounds) to pull down captured and wounded animals. The
deer bed in cover on lower ground. On the morning of the hunt, beaters and
dog handlers with hounds leashed together in couples flank the herd on either
side of a valley and a party of hunters and dogs begin to drive the deer toward
bowmen hidden along their path in covered stands or "stables." The deer at-
tempt to scatter, but the beaters turn them back, except for the stags, which they
let escape. Only does were hunted in winter.

    Once the deer are moving in the desired direction, the dog handlers "slip" or
uncouple their hounds, and the horsemen trailing the herd drive them ahead
so the bowmen can shoot them down. Any deer that survive this ambush and

The brachets[68] all bayed with brave belling voices,
But the men beat them back, those who would bolt,
A full hundred hunters as I have since heard,
>   steadfast.   1145
>   The handlers reach their marks,
>   And now the hounds are cast!
>   Loud bugling fills the park;
>   The forest rings with blasts!

The wild creatures quaked at the calling and clamor.   1150
Deer dashed through the dale, half-maddened with dread.
They bolted up braes, but turned back at the tops,
Rebuffed by the beaters who bawled in their faces.
The men let the harts[69] pass, those bearing high horns,
The bold bucks bounding beneath their broad antlers.   1155
Their lord counted it crime in the coldest of seasons
For a man of his household to maim a male deer,
But the hinds were held in with "Hey!" and "Beware!"
And driven with din to the depths of the dale.
There you might see, as men slipped their swift shafts,   1160
At each fold of the forest the bright flash of arrows
That bit the brown hides with their broad, sharpened heads.
Wah! The deer brayed and bled by the banks as they died,
Harried by hounds driven wild by the hunt
And the hunters with horns on their hastening mounts.   1165
Such clangor! Such calling! The cliffs might have burst!
Those hinds that eluded the hurrying hunters
Were seen and brought down at the hides built below,
Shut off from the hills they splashed through streams.
The lords shot with skill from their stands near the water,   1170
And the greathearted dogs gripped does like grim death,
Hauling them down while their handlers looked on,
>   rare sight.

---

another line of blinds farther down across the mouth of the valley may be pulled
down by the greyhounds and mounted hunters.

68. Pack hounds.

69. Males, like the bucks at line 1155. Females were called *hinds*.

The lord laughed out in glee,
And rode with reckless might,   1175
Throughout the day full free,
And so to dark of night.

Thus larks the lord by the linden-wood's eaves,
While Gawain, the good warrior, waits in his bed,
Lying late till the daylight gleamed on the walls,   1180
Beneath a comfortable coverlet, well curtained about.
As he lay half in slumber, he heard a slight sound—
A small din at his door—and saw it draw open.
He heaves up his head, out of the bedclothes,
And curls back a corner of the curtain a little,   1185
While warily watching for what it might be.
Lo! The lord's winsome lady, and never more lovely!
She drew the door shut, all silent and still,
And bent toward the bed. Gawain, quite abashed,
Lay back to mislead her, like one long asleep.   1190
She slipped across soundlessly, stole to his bedstead,
Cast up the curtain, and crept in herself!
She set herself softly on the side of the bed,
And lingered at length there to look for his waking.
He lay low a while, aligning his thoughts,   1195
Casting in conscience what her coming could mean
And what else might happen—a wonder he held it!
But he said to himself, "Far more seemly it were
To tell by her talk what the lady intends."
So he started and stretched and swung toward her side.   1200
Unlocking his eyelids, he lurched like one startled
And signed himself swiftly as if shriving his soul
                    in dread.
        Her cheeks shone all the while
        With mingled white and red.   1205
        Her lips half-hid a smile,
        That lovely on his bed.

"Good morrow, good man," said the mild lady gaily,
"You are too sound a sleeper, to let one slip in so.

You're taken, sir, totally. Now treat for a truce   1210
Or be bound in your bed. Believe me, you will be."
She laughed as she launched her light, teasing words.
"Good morrow, good madam," said Gawain, just as merry,
"I shall work as you wish, and willingly, too.
I capitulate promptly, appeal for your grace.   1215
It is best, I believe, to obey as I should."
Thus he talked in his turn with quick touches of laughter.
"But, loveliest lady, if you'd lend me your leave
And unpinion your prisoner and pray him stand up,
I'd come forth from these covers and clothe myself rightly   1220
To appear to you properly and parley at will."
"Not so, my good sir," was the sweet lady's answer,
"You shan't budge from that bed. No, I'll rule you much better.
You'll be bundled in blankets—before and behind—
And thus I'll converse with my captured companion,   1225
For I know well enough you're that noble Gawain,
Whom all the world worships wherever you go.
Your conscience, your courtesy are commonly praised
Among ladies and lords and all who bear life.
And now, sir, you lie here. We're left all alone.   1230
My lord and his fellows ride far through the fields.
The servants are snoring, my maidens asleep.
The door is well drawn, done up with a bolt.
Since I have in this house one whom all the world dotes on,
I shall seize on the moment and savor your speech   1235
          today.
          Lo, I am yours, my lord,
          So use me as you may.
          I'll not be untoward,
          Your servant in each way.   1240

"On my word," said Gawain, "I welcome this offer,
Though I'm hardly the hero of whom you are speaking.
The gracious regard that you've given me here
Is more than I'm worth, as I'm well aware.
By God, I'd be glad, if you thought it were good,   1245

To set my full mind, in my speech or my service,
To please one so praiseworthy—a pleasure indeed."
"My word, Sir Gawain," the winsome one answered,
"Your price and your prowess are everywhere praised;
To lower or lessen them would be impolite.   1250
There are legions of ladies who'd like nothing more
Than to have you in their hold, sir—as I have you here—
To dally and deal with and dwell on your words,
Acquiring good comfort and cooling their cares;
They'd give all they've got for you, treasure and gold.   1255
But thanks to the Lord who leads our poor lives,
I have wholly in hand what all others desire,
                    through grace.
        She poured forth her allure,
        Who was so fair of face.   1260
        The knight with speeches pure
        Made answer in each case.

"Madam," he said merrily, "may Mary reward you,
For I've found you full free, in good faith, and right noble.
Others may win men's good words for their works,   1265
But my name as a knight owes nothing to me;
It comes from your courtesy. You're too kind by far."
"On my oath," said the other, "I hardly agree.
If I were first of all women alive in the world,
And wielded at will all the wealth I could wish,   1270
And could choose as I cared to the comeliest lord,
For the worth that I've witnessed, Gawain, in yourself,
Of beauty and breeding and brightness of semblance,
And all that I've heard of you, and hold for the truth,
There's no manner of man who could move me but you."   1275
"But, all worthy," Gawain said, "you're wed to one better!
Yet I'm proud of the price you apportion me here.
I'm surely your servant and hold you my sovereign
And name me your knight—may God grant you grace."
They tarried there talking until midmorning tide,   1280
And ever the lady let on that she loved him.

He spoke to her smoothly, while saving his honor.
And though no lady was lovelier, the lord had indeed
A worse will to be wooing for the wound he must seek,
           no boon.   1285
     That dint brooked no reprieve,
     The knight must needs be hewn;
     And when she took her leave,
     He let her go full soon.

She gave him good day, glancing back with a laugh,   1290
But caused him to smart with some sharp-spoken words.
"May He who speeds speech requite you," she said,
"But I'm loath to believe, lord, that you are Gawain!"
"And why?" good Gawain warily asks her,
Fearing he'd failed in some fashion or act.   1295
The bright lady blessed him, but baited him too:
"One so good as Gawain is given to be,
Enclosing all courtliness clasped in himself,
Could not linger so lightly and long with a lady
Without craving a kiss, sir—courtesy calls for it—   1300
By some touch or some trifling turn of his talk."
"Well," said Gawain, "I shall work as you wish,
And kiss on command as becomes a good knight,
For fear of offending, so ask me no further."
At that she comes closer and clips him in arms,   1305
Leans down all lovely and kisses his lips.
They courteously commit one another to Christ,
And she goes on her way without wasting more words.
He rises up readily, and rushing about
Calls to his chamberlain, chooses his clothes,   1310
And hurries forth happy to hear that day's Mass.
Then after his meal, which men had kept waiting,
He made merry among them until the moon rose,
           with cheer.
     No knight was treated better,   1315
     By ladies far or near.
     The old and young together,
     Both held the good knight dear.

Just as late the lord of the land held his hunt,
Harrying holt and heath after hinds.   1320
Such a swarm did he slay before the sun set
Of does and such deer, you would deem it a wonder.
Then the hunters hastily hauled up their game,
And heaped the dead hinds in a handsome display.[70]
Lords and their liegemen alighted there first   1325
And fell on the fleshiest deer they could find
To carve them correctly as custom commanded.
Some set themselves to assay the deer's fat:
Two fingers they found on the frailest of carcasses.[71]
Then they slashed the deer's throats and groped for
        their gullets,[72]   1330
Shaved them out with sharp knives and knotted them off.
They lopped off the limbs and loosened the hides,
And then breached the deer's bellies and brought forth
        the bowels,[73]
Taking care not to cut through the knots that confined them.
Next, they gripped the deer's gorges to skillfully part   1335
Gullets and windpipes, and groped out the guts.
They sheared out the shoulders with sharply honed knives,
Severing them inside to save the skin whole,
And took blades to the breasts to break them in two.
Then again at the gullet one strikes a new gash,   1340
Slices down to the forelegs for liver and lights,[74]
Pulls out these front parts, and promptly thereafter

---

70. It was customary to lay out the day's kill and divide the quarry. Local lords
and dignitaries of the hunt had first choice with the help of an *assay* to tell which
were the fattest, best-conditioned deer.

71. The fat went as deep as two fingers laid side to side. A very good amount.

72. "Breaking" beasts was a gentlemanly art. The details here are not as clearly
explained as they might be, but the author's careful description shows that
butchering game was a ritual with carefully prescribed rules and terminology.

73. A deer's diaphragm divides its internal organs into two parts: the digestive
tract toward the rear and the liver, lungs, heart, and other organs toward the
front. These are kept separate as the animal is butchered.

74. The deer's lights are their lungs.

They remove the thin membranes made fast to the ribs,
Cutting them carefully clear of the backbone,
Down to the haunches, to hasp round the offal   1345
And heave it up whole and hew the mass free.
They name this the numbles, who know of this art
                    by kind.
            Where the haunches meet
            They carve them off behind.   1350
            Then split the backbone neat,
            The foreparts to unbind.

They hewed off the heads and the heavy necks with them,
And then swiftly sundered the sides from the spine,
Cast the bone for the corbies in a copse of young trees,[75]   1355
And struck each thick side through by the ribs.
These they hung high by the hocks of the forelegs
Until each man is dealt his due parts of the deer.[76]
They feed their good hounds on the hide of a hind
With the livers and lungs and leathery stomachs   1360
And bread soaked in blood well blended with these.
Then they bugle the kill as the brachets bawl round them,
And truss up their trophies and take their way home,
Blowing bold horn blasts ahead as they ride.
The light barely lingered when the last lord arrived   1365
At the company's castle where the courtier sits
                    at rest.
            Before a fire well set
            The lord salutes his guest.
            When those two nobles met,   1370
            Goodwill filled each man's breast.

---

75. A bit of gristle from the brisket reserved for the crows and ravens (corbies) that followed the hunt.

76. Each hunter came in for a share of the meat as defined, once again, by custom. High lords got the bulk of the carcass, while footmen and beaters shared the backbones and necks.

The sire then assembled his house in the hall,
Both ladies as well, along with their maids.
Before those folk on the floor he orders his men
To display his day's doings—the does he destroyed—   1375
And gaily in game he goes to Gawain,
Tells him to tally the carcasses there,
And shows him the fat that was shorn from their sides.
"What say you?" he asks. "Have I shone at this sport?
Have I given you cause to acclaim me for woodcraft?"   1380
"Aye," said the other, "I've beheld no such kill
These seven years in the wintery season."
"I yield all this to you," said his host, the good sire.
"Our accord and high covenant calls for as much."
"Just so," said Gawain, "and I say the same: 1385
Whatever I won in these walls is your own,
So I offer it up now with equal goodwill."
He hales his fair host fast in his arms
And kisses him as keenly as he could contrive.
"Now you've got my day's gains. I garnered no more.   1390
I'd give them up gladly even if they were greater."
"They're ample," his host said. "I'm obliged to you, sir;
But I'd be yet more pleased if you would explain
How you won all this wealth. By your wit, I suppose?"
"That's no part of my pledge," said Gawain, "so don't press me.   1395
You've got all you should; don't guess something more
                    is due."
          They laughed then and made gay
          With courteous words and true,
          Then supped without delay,   1400
          On many dainties new.

And then by the chamber's warm chimney they sat
With wine of the best that men brought to the board.
Among their amusements, they agree that in the morning
They'd repeat the same pledge that they'd plighted before: 1405
What each chanced to achieve they'd accord to the other,
All they obtained would be traded that night.

They proclaim their new compact before the whole court.
A bumper was brought in to bless their new bargain;
Then the levy took leave of each other at last;   1410
And the lords and their ladies went lightly to bed.
Now, the castle's cocks had not crowed more than thrice
When the host and his huntsmen heaved up awake.
Once their meat and devotions were duly dispatched,
They met on the moors before morning had broken,   1415
        to chase.
    Hunters and loud horns
    Fly through the fields apace.
    Uncoupled, through the thorns
    Their brachets gaily race.   1420

Soon they seize on a scent by the side of a marsh.
Hunters hailed the keen hounds that took hold of it first,
Whooping wild words through the woods as they went.
The other dogs heard them and hastened together
To follow the track, full forty at once.   1425
Such bellows and baying babbled up then
That the rocks fairly rang as dogs ran on the trail
While the hunters hied after with horns and loud urging.
When all were assembled, they sped in a swarm
Between a tarn in the trees and a towering crag.   1430
In the brush by a bank beneath the tall cliff,
Where rough rocks had rolled into unruly heaps,
The hounds bawled a find, and the hunt stopped for breath.
They spread round the spinney surrounding the cliff,
Well aware of what waited within that wild lair—   1435
The beast that the bloodhounds betrayed with their braying.
When men beat on the bushes and bid him come out,
He boiled out of the brake and brushed them aside:
The world's brawniest boar broke through their lines.
Single and savage he'd survived on his own,   1440
A fell swine and furious, the fiercest on ground,
Greathearted, loud-grunting, and grievous to many.
His first charge felled three fellows flat to the earth;
Then he sped off despite them, despoiling no more.

They hallooed him mightily, with *huzzahs* and *heys*,　　　1445
Haled horns to their mouths and blew hasty calls.
Merry howls rose to heaven from hounds and from men,
Rushing after the boar with bellows and horn blasts
　　　to kill.
　　Often he stops at bay　　　1450
　　And maims dogs as he will;
　　The hounds part in his way.
　　They yowl and cringe and mill.

Now archers hasten to harass him with bows,
They strike him with arrows, often and hard.　　　1455
But the points could not pierce the pith of his shoulders,
And no barb would bite on his bristling brows.
The smoothly shaped shafts shivered to pieces,
While the heads skittered off, wherever they hit.
The swine sweltered with rage beneath their sharp blows,　　　1460
And then maddened and murderous he rushes the men,
Slashes them savagely and speeds on his way.
Not a few were afraid and fell back before him,
But the sire on his stallion rides swift on his trail.
Bright-hearted and brave, he sounds his bold bugle　　　1465
To hearten the hunt as he hied through the trees,
Chasing the swine till the sun shone aslant.
The day and its doings drew on in this way,
While our lovesome knight lingers long in his bed,
At ease in the castle, wrapped in costly, warm covers,　　　1470
　　　dyed bright.
　　The lady did not forget
　　To try him as she might.
　　She came full early, set
　　To captivate the knight.　　　1475

Drawing up to the curtain, she casts him a look.
Sir Gawain bid her welcome at once, most politely,
And she pertly replies to the prince with kind words.
She sits herself softly beside him and laughs;
With love in her looks, she launches her speech:　　　1480

"Sir, if you're Gawain, I rate it a wonder—
A knight who's so noble, enamored of good,
And yet can't comprehend what courtesy calls for;
And if someone should show you, you set it aside!
To lose sight so soon of the schooling I gave you,   1485
With the most loving lesson a lady can lend!"
"What was that?" said the knight. "In God's name,
    I don't know.
If you're judging me justly, I'm to blame, and no jest."
"But I discoursed of kissing!" the lady exclaimed.
"Where a kiss is forthcoming, you must crave it at once.   1490
That becomes any knight who claims to be courteous."
"My lady," the lord said, "leave off such speech.
I'd never dare ask, lest you should grow angry.
The request would be rude if it earned a rebuff."
"My faith," said the fair one, "you need fear no refusal,   1495
You could compel kisses by strength should you choose—
That's if some headstrong she should wickedly shun you!"
"By God," said Gawain, "that's a good way to talk!
Threats never thrive with those where I dwell,
Nor gifts that are given with less than goodwill.   1500
Yet I'm yours to command. Kiss away if you care to.
Work as you wish and leave off when you like,
                apace."
        The lady then bends down
        To sweetly kiss his face,   1505
        And next the two expound
        On love's sharp pangs and grace.

"I would learn from you, lord," said the lady at length,
"If you'd not be annoyed, the nature of this:
How so lissome and lively and youthful a lord   1510
And a more noble or knightly one never was known—
When the chief point of chivalry, choicest of all,
Is loyally to love—a knight's highest lore. . . .
Sir, the tale of the toils of the truest of knights,
The title and token and text of their works,   1515
Is how loving, good lords have ventured their lives,

Endured for their dear ones the direst of trials,
Evincing their valor and voiding her care,
And brought bliss to her bower by acting so bravely. . . .
Now, you're known as the noblest knight of your age,   1520
Your worth and your worship are widely extolled,
Yet I've sat by your side two separate times
And have yet to hear you offer one word
Belonging to love—not the least little hint!
One so polite and so prompt to give pledges   1525
Ought to be eager to help a young girl
And teach her some terms of true lover's talk.
Are you unschooled yourself, despite your great fame?
Or do you deem me too dull for such dalliance, sir?
          How queer!   1530
      I come alone and sit,
      To learn love's game, my dear.
      Do teach me of your wit,
      Now that my lord's not here."

"My word," said Gawain, "God yield you reward!   1535
Great is the joy you're so good, dear, to give me,
That one worthy as you would wend her way here,
And pain you to play with a poor knight like me,
And with so kind a countenance! It comforts me well.
But to take on this trial—to truly expound   1540
And teach you the terms found in tales of romance—
When you, I know well, wield far wider skill
In that art than I, or a hundred such men
As I am, or will be, while here on this earth. . . .
It were folly, dear friend, fiftyfold, by my truth.   1545
Yet I'll accede to your asking as far as I'm able,
For I'm highly beholden, and will evermore be
Your suitor and servant, and so save me God!"
Thus the lady assayed him and sounded him steadily
To move him to mischief, and more if she might.   1550
But his defense was so fair and faultless indeed
That neither trespassed, though they played as they pleased
          in bliss.

They laughed and chatted long.
Yet nothing went amiss;   1555
Till, neither in the wrong,
She gave him one more kiss.

The knight stirs himself, proceeding to Mass,
And broke his night's fast with good fare finely served.
Gawain and the ladies relaxed then at length,   1560
While his stalwart host hurtled headlong on his hunt,
Pursuing the boar as it bolts through the beech wood,
Biting the backs of his brachets in two.
It would brave them at bay, until bowmen appeared
To make the swine scurry in spite of himself,   1565
So sharp were the shafts they sent skimming against him.
Yet he beat back the boldest ones, breaking away,
Till he spent all his force and could flee no farther.
With what speed he could summon he makes for a stand,
On a rock rearing over a fast-rushing torrent.   1570
He puts his back to a scarp and scrapes out his spot.
An ugly froth foamed at the folds of his mouth
As he whet his white tusks. They were wary of him,
Those wholehearted hunters beholding him there.
They shot from the stream side, but none would step closer,   1575
                all loath.
        He'd hurt so many then
        That none dared, on my oath,
        To face his tusks again,
        So fierce and brainsick both—   1580

Till the host came on hand, spurring his horse,
He sees the bayed swine standing off his good huntsmen
And lights down full lightly, loosing his mount.
He bares his bright brand and boldly strides forth
Through the ford to the fold where the fell boar was waiting, 1585
As it watched the man wade with weapon in hand,
Its hackles rose high, and it grunted so hotly
They feared for the lord lest the worst fate befall him.

The boar charges boldly and bowls the man over,
So that swordsman and swine are swept in a heap   1590
In the welter of water—the worse for the pig,
For the man marked him well upon their first meeting,
Aimed his blade at the breast by the base of his neck,
And drove it in to the hilt to splinter the heart.
The swine twisted away and tossed dead down the torrent,   1595
> their prize.
>> The brachets seize the boar
>> With teeth and frantic cries.
>> Men roll his bulk ashore.
>> The hounds yelp his demise.   1600

They honored the hunted with horn calls and shouts
Hallooing on high, those hunters who could.
Brachets bayed for the beast as their masters bid them—
The chief men who managed that challenging chase.
And then one man full wise in the ways of the woods   1605
Bent to the work of breaking the boar.
First he hews off the head and sets it on high,[77]
And splits him in half by the side of the spine.
He brings out the bowels and broils them on coals
And blends them with bread for the brachets' reward.   1610
Then he slices off slabs of the savory flesh
And lifts out the liver and kidneys and lights.
He hasps the two halves into one once again
To hoist them up high on a heavy wood pole.
Now they catch up the carcass to carry it home.   1615
The boar's head was borne before the brave sire
Who finished the fray by the force of his hands,
> so true.
>> He's thinking of Gawain
>> And growing eager too,   1620
>> To reach his home again
>> And learn what he is due.

---

77. Probably on a staff or pole.

The lord, with loud laughter and light, gamesome words,
When he sees Sir Gawain, speaks to him gaily.
The ladies were summoned, the servants assembled.   1625
He shows them the swine flesh and tells them the story:
The largeness and length and relentless hot rage
Of the boar that they battled at bay in the woods.
His courtly companion commended his deeds,
And praised his prowess, well proved in that hunt.   1630
No brawnier beast, or bigger, he said,
Nor such sides of sweet swine flesh, had he ever seen.
When they handled the hog's head, he hailed that as well,
Heightening his horror to honor the lord.
"Now, Gawain," said the good man, "this game is your own   1635
By the terms of our treaty, as truly you know."
"Aye," said the hero, "and you can be sure
That I'll give you my own gains again, by my faith."
He took the host in his arms and heartily kissed him,
Then one more of the same he served the man, saying,   1640
"And now we are even, sir, this eventide.
We've kept all the contracts we knit in your court,
                    full fair."
        The lord said, "By Saint Giles,
        Sir, you're the best, I swear!   1645
        If you go on in this style,
        You'll be rich beyond compare!"

Then tops went on trestles to make tables for dining.[78]
Men laid on the linen, and watched the clear light
Wake on the walls beneath the waxed torches.   1650
Servants set silver and served up the supper.
Rejoicing and revelry rang through the place,
Around the great hearth and all through the hall,
Both at mealtime and after, with many fine songs—
Carols from Christmas and cunning new dances—   1655

---

78. Tables—folding trestles and tops—were set up for each meal. At other times
the hall was largely free of furniture.

And the most matchless mirth that a man might relate.
Gawain sat and watched by the winning wife's side.
Such a sweet semblance she showed to her knight,
Such sly, stolen glances sent for his comfort,
That he was perplexed and in good part displeased.   1660
Still, too well bred to rebuff her or not to glance back,
He repaid her courteously, though it could have been counted
                            unfit.
        Those two played in this vein
        Till they were pleased to quit,   1665
        And the lord signed to Gawain
        To come away and sit.

Then by the lord's fire it fared as before:
They repeated their pledges to proclaim the new year.
The honest knight asked to be off once again,   1670
For the time of his testing was truly at hand.
But the lord bade him linger yet longer instead,
Saying, "Sir, rest assured now; I swear by my truth
You'll achieve the Green Chapel and accomplish your chore
By the light of the new year, and long before prime,[79]   1675
So now lie in your loft here and laze at your ease.
I shall hunt through the holts and hold to our pact:
Trade trophy for trophy when I return home;
For I've tested you twice and found you right truthful,
Yet 'The third throw tells all.' Think of that, sir, tomorrow. 1680
While we may, let's be merry and mindful of pleasure,
For sorrows come swiftly as soon as we call them."
This was gracefully granted and Gawain's stay prolonged.
They shared a last bumper then went bedward with brands,
                            so bright.   1685
        Sir Gawain slumbers sound,
        Still and soft all night.
        But the lord, on hunting bound,
        Was up before first light.

―――――――
79. About six a.m.

After Mass and a morsel for master and men,   1690
The morning dawned mild as he called for his mount.
All the hunters, well horsed to follow the hounds,
Sat in their saddles outside the hall door.
Frosted white with the winter, the woods lay before them.
Ruddy red the sun rises through runnels of mist   1695
To coast high and clear past thin clouds in the sky.
Hunters loosed hounds by the side of a holt,
And made the rocks ring with their riotous horns.
The tossing hounds took up the trail of a fox,
Casting across it to catch every turn.   1700
An ebullient beagle soon bawls to the hunters.
His fast-panting fellows followed him closely,
Running forth in a rabble to rend the sly fox.
The frightened beast flees. They drive him before them.
At the sight of him scampering, they stiffened their pace, 1705
Deriding him roughly with rancorous yawps.
He dodged them and darted down through rough tangles,
Lingering to listen alongside each hedge.
At length, though, he leaps in a ditch lined with thorns
And steals out by stealth to the side of a marsh.   1710
He thought that his tricks had taken them in,
But he went unaware by a well-hidden stand
Where watchers were waiting with three more tough hounds,
    all gray.
   The fleet fox dodged aside   1715
   And darted on his way.
   In great fear for his hide,
   He hardly cared to stay.

Ah, then it was heaven to hark as the hounds,
In a gang once again, all gathered together,   1720
Decried the poor creature, creating a sound
As if clusters of cliffs had come clapping down!
Here, hunters hallooed him, hide as he may,
Calling and chiding with callous, hard words.
There, he was threatened, told out for a thief,   1725
With hounds' teeth at his tail, and no time to tarry.

They were there to attack when he turned to the open,
Skirring and scudding—resourceful Reynard![80]
While the fox led the lord and his liegemen along
Amid the rough mountains till midday was past,   1730
Gawain slept wonderfully, as well as he would,
In comfort, with curtains to keep out the cold.
But the lady, for love, could not linger in slumber,
Nor put by the purpose that prickled her heart.
She roused herself early and went to his room,   1735
In a finely made mantle that fell to the floor,
Well lined with furs, formed and finished with skill,
No cloth for her head, but a cluster of gems
Traced through her tresses, twenty together.
From her face to her forefront her fair skin shone naked,   1740
Her breast bare before her, her back bare as well.
She enters his door and hasps it behind her,
Opens a window and hails the good knight.
He rapidly rouses at her ready words
                                and cheer.   1745
            "Ah, man, why lie abed
            When morning dawns so clear?"
        Though dire dreams filled his head,
        He cannot fail to hear.

He was deep in his drowsing, dreaming and muttering   1750
Like a man cast in mourning by many ill thoughts—
How next day his destiny should deal him his fate
When he came to the chapel and encountered his foe
To abide the man's blow, nor try to rebuff it.
But at the comely one's coming, he caught up his wits.   1755
He starts up from slumber and answers her soon.
All lovely, the lady came laughing and sweet,
To bend close to his face and cordially kiss him.
He welcomed her worthily with winning good cheer.
When he sees her so sportive and splendidly dressed,   1760
So faultless of feature, in fine, blooming color,

---

80. Conventional name for a fox.

Joy welled up at once, and woe quit his heart.
With smooth words and smiles they slipped into mirth.
All that passed there between them was polished and pleasant
              and bright.   1765
    They discoursed as they would,
    And both grew gay and light.
    Great peril between them stood
    Should Mary forsake her knight.

For that pleasing, rare princess pressed him so closely,   1770
Urged him so ardently up to the edge,
He must reply to her passion or rudely repel it.
He cared for his courtesy—he'd not seem uncouth—
But more for the mischief should he commit sin
And harm his good host who held that fine castle: 1775
"God deny it," the knight said, "that never must be!"
With a little light laughter he laid to one side
All the love-talk and longing that sprang from her lips.
"My lord, you're to blame," the lady said then,
"If you won't love a lady who lies by your side—   1780
Wounded at heart beyond any on earth—
Unless you've a lover whose love you prefer,
And your faith is so firm and fastened to her
You're loath now to loosen it, as I must believe.
If that's true, sir, then tell me in straightforward terms.   1785
By all lovers alive, do not lie to me now
           with guile."
    The knight said, "By the sun,"
    And offered her a smile,
    "In faith, no, I have none,   1790
    Nor will I for some while."

"That word," said the woman, "could hardly be worse,
But you've answered me honestly, though I think it sore.
Kiss me now, kindly, and I'll quit your room
To mourn evermore, as one much in love."   1795
Saddened and sighing, she stoops for his kiss;

Then standing beside him she says to the knight,
"Dear, I pray at this parting you please me in this:
Give me some gift—your glove would suffice—
A souvenir, sir, to soften my grief."   1800
"Ah, well," said Gawain, "I wish I had here
The worthiest thing I wield in the world.
You deserve that for certain, and much more besides,
A richer reward than I, dear, can reach to.
But to give as a love-gift some gear of no worth!   1805
It would hardly sit well with your honor to have
A glove or poor gewgaw-like gift from Gawain.
And I'm here on an errand away from my home,
With no servants or stores of presentable keepsakes.
I lament it, my lady, and most for your love,   1810
But we must do as we're destined to. Don't deem it amiss
          or pine."
     "Lord, all you say is true,"
     She replied in robes full fine;
     "But though I've naught from you,   1815
     Please have a jot of mine."

She held out a rich ring worked in red gold
With a sumptuous stone that stood up full proud,
Scattering sparkles as bright as the sun.
It was worth, if you wish, a huge price in the world,   1820
But the good knight denied it, nobly saying,
"No, no gifts, for God's sake, gay lady, for me.
I have nothing to give and so naught will I take."
She prodded and pressed him but could not prevail:
He claimed by his soul he couldn't accept it.   1825
His words seemed to sadden her. Swiftly she said,
"If you're refusing my ring, sir, for fear it's too rich,
And you don't want to fall so deep in my debt,
I'll give you my girdle,[81] though you'll gain that much less."
She smoothly unlatched a sash round her sides,   1830

---

81. Her sash.

Gathering the gown that gleamed under her mantle—
A silk girdle of green well garnished with gold
On its brightly stitched borders and beautiful fringes.
This she offered her friend and freely besought him,
Though its worth was less weighty, to welcome the gift.   1835
But he set it by, saying he couldn't accept
Gold nor rich gauds until God sent him grace
To achieve the hard chore he had chosen to try.
"I beseech you," he said, "don't be distressed.
Give over your urging, this hope that I cannot   1840
     fulfill.
     I'm in your debt fourfold
     Because of your goodwill.
     And ever, hot or cold,
     I'll be your servant still."   1845

"Do you scorn my poor sash?" said the lady. "For shame!
You suppose it's too simple? It seems so indeed.
You may think as it's little, the less is its worth.
Yet any who knew what is knit in this girdle
Might prize it more highly, as precious, perhaps;   1850
For while one is wrapped in this web of green silk,
Having the sash fastened aptly about him,
No hero on earth can hurt him or maim him,
For he cannot be slain by skill or by sleight."
Gawain felt a wonder awake in his heart.   1855
Here was a gem for the game he'd engaged in!
If he achieved the Green Chapel and suffered his chance,
And yet slipped off unslain, what a sleight that would be!
Then he listened more leniently, let her speak longer.
And she praised her bright present, pressing it on him.   1860
He agreed, and she granted the gift with goodwill,
Yet besought for her sake he never would show it,
But keep it hid from her husband. The hero consents,
Promising no one would know that he had it
     but they.   1865
     He thanked her as he could,
     His warm heart full and gay,

And full three kisses good
She gave the knight that day.

Then she bids him goodbye and tends to her business,   1870
For she'd got all the mirth that she might from the man.
When she was gone Gawain gathers his gear,
Rises, gets ready in noble array.
He laid up the love-lace the lady had given him,
Artfully hid it where he alone knew.   1875
Then quickly to chapel he chooses his way,
Privately spoke to a priest there and prayed
He would hear his confession and inform him in full
How his soul should be saved when his body was spent.
The knight shrived himself surely and showed his misdeeds—   1880
Major and minor sins—beseeching God's mercy.
He prayed for forgiveness, imploring the priest,
Who absolved all his sins and sent him forth clean
As if Doomsday were destined to dawn the next morning.
He left to make merry with those lovesome ladies   1885
With the comeliest carols and best kinds of joy
As never before from noon until night,
                    I vow.
        He gave them such delight.
        Both ladies said, "Somehow,   1890
        He's never shone more bright
        Since he's been here than now!"

Now let's leave Sir Gawain, may love long delight him,
For the lord of the land is still leading his hunt,
And he's headed the fox he spurred after so long.   1895
As he sprang through a spinney to spy the wretch out,
Reynard stole his way through a web of thick woods.
The fox heard the hounds howling behind him—
All that brabbling rabble right on his heels!
The lord sees the wily one and warily waits,   1900
Then unsheathes his bright sword to swipe at the beast.
The fox shrank from the stroke and tried to swerve back.
A dog catches him dodging. He's down in a trice.

By the horse's front hooves the hounds swarm and heave
To worry the wild one with earsplitting wrath.   1905
The lord dismounts lightly to lift the remains,
Raising him rapidly out of reach of those mouths.
He holds him high overhead and whoops with delight
As the brachets boil round him, baying the death.
The hunt galloped toward them with echoing horns,   1910
To rally the riders to rein closer in.
All the coursers recalled, they convened on the spot.
Each man with a bugle blew blast upon blast,
While any without one bellowed, "*Halloo!*"
It was the merriest mort that a man ever heard,   1915
The ruckus they raised for the soul of Reynard,
> each throat!
>> They give their hounds reward.
>> They pat the dogs and gloat,
>> Then roughly seize the fox   1920
>> And strip away his coat.

Next they headed for home, for evening was nigh,
Striking out stoutly with dissonant horns.
The lord feels full light in the castle he loves
With a fine fire before him, his friend there as well—   1925
Sir Gawain the Good, gladdened and gay,
And languid with ladies and love and enjoyment.
Both his robe of blue silk reaching down to the ground
And his seemly, furred surcoat suited him well,
While a hood of the same hung soft from his shoulders,   1930
All bordered in ermine, white bands pure and bright.
He hails his good host midway in the hall,
Graciously giving the man a fair greeting.
"I shall hastily yield what I owe you," he says,
"As we properly pledged, sir, with plenty of drink."   1935
Then he clasps his good host and accords him three kisses
With all the sweetness and savor that he could supply.
"God's love!" said the lord, "You've been lucky indeed
To garner such goods if you got them right cheap!"

"We won't weigh their prices," Gawain said at once;   1940
"Be pleased that I've paid you the profits I owed."
"Marry!"[82] the host said, "How I am behind,
For I've hunted all day without gaining aught
But the skin of a fox—the fiend take his fur!
Small reward, I'm aware, for such wondrous things   1945
As you generously gave me—a gracious three kisses,
                so good."
        "By the cross," said Sir Gawain,
        "I thank you as I should."
        And how the fox was slain   1950
        He heard there as they stood.

With mirth and with minstrelsy and meat at their will,
They made themselves merry as any men might,
With laughing of ladies and light-spoken jests.
Gawain and the good lord both grew as glad   1955
As if they were dizzy or drunk on strong wine.
Both the lord and his liegemen laughed and made japes
Till the time was upon them when they must retire.
Sleep beckoned the boldest to bed at the last.
First the hero took leave of his greathearted host,   1960
Beholden and honored, he offered him thanks:
"For the gentle, good sojourn that I've enjoyed here,
And my keep over Christmas, may good Christ repay you.
Take my service now, lord, for the loan of one liegeman,
For I must leave here at last, as you know, lord, tomorrow.   1965
Please grant me the guide you promised to give me
To lead me to this chapel, if the Lord will allow it,
To greet the new year undergoing my fate."
"On my honor," his host said, "with all my goodwill.
What I plighted and promised, I'll perform ere we part."   1970
He assigns him a servant to see him well sped,
To fare through the fells with no frets or delays,

---

82. Mild euphemism for "Mary," the mother of Christ.

To traverse the wild copses and cut straight across
       each dell.
     Gawain now thanks the lord   1975
     For hosting him so well
     And then with fair accord
     Of the ladies takes farewell.

With care and with kissing he compliments them,
Pressing his praise on the pair as they part.   1980
And the two of them gave him as good as they got.
Each commends him to Christ with care and keen sighs.
From all of the household he asks their good leave.
To each man he met, he made his last thanks
For his comfort and solace while kept in their care,   1985
How they busily bustled about in his service.
It pained all those people to part with Gawain
As if they'd known the good lord as long as they'd lived.
Then they led him with lights to lie in his chamber;
They brought him full blithely to bed there to rest.   1990
How soundly he slept I hardly could say,
For he had much the next morning to mind if he would,
         in thought.
     Let him lie there as he will;
     He's near the thing he sought.   1995
     Now, if you'll all be still,
     I'll tell you how they wrought.

PART 4

NOW the New Year draws nigh as night fades away.
Day drives off the dark as Destiny bids,
But wild, wintry weather awakened outside: 2000
Clouds cast the keen, crackling cold to the earth
With North Wind enough to numb naked wretches.
Snow sleeted aslant, stinging wild beasts.
The weltering wind whipped the world from on high,
Driving each dale full of drift-piles of snow. 2005
Gawain listened well, awake in his bed,
Though his eyelids are locked, full little he sleeps,
By each cock as it crowed, he counted the hours.
He rapidly rose ere morning had reddened
By the glints of a lamp left alight in the room, 2010
And summoned his servant, who answered him shortly,
To hand him his hauberk and saddle his horse.
The good man goes out to gather his gear
And dresses Gawain in the worthiest way.
First he enclosed him in warm clothes to keep out the cold, 2015
Then he added the war harness he had in his care:
Bright pieces of plate, polished full clean,
And his mail, with each ring of it rubbed free of rust.
All his fittings shone flawless, and the knight offered thanks
          perforce. 2020
    When he'd put on every piece,
    Well cleansed and wiped by course,
    The best knight from here to Greece
    Sent one to fetch his horse.

Then he wrapped himself well in his most regal robe: 2025
His surcoat was set with a sumptuous badge,

Vibrant on velvet, with virtuous stones,
Bound and embellished and richly embroidered,
And finished within with the finest of furs.
But he left not the lace, the lady's last gift.   2030
He'd hardly forgo that and hazard his health.
When he'd belted his brand about his strong haunches,
He gathered the girdle twice round his girth,
Quickly and rightly wrapping it round him,
That sash of green silk that suited him well   2035
Where it shimmered and shone on its setting of red.
But Gawain hardly wore it to show off his wealth,
Or for pride of its pendants, though polished and bright,
Nor the glittering gold that gleamed on its fringes,
But to shield his fair skin, when suffer he should,   2040
Awaiting a wound with no warding of sword
                or blade.
        So fitly dressed again,
        He returns to his true trade.
        To all his host's good men,   2045
        His thanks were freely paid.

Then was Gringolet girt, that great horse and huge.
Who'd been stoutly stabled, safe and secure.
He pranced in his place, well pleased to be going.
Gawain found him fit, in fine coat and flesh,   2050
And full soft to himself he swore on his truth:
"This castle and court are mindful of courtesy;
With the one who upholds them may they all go in joy!
And as for the lady, may love fill her life.
If kindness causes them to cosset a guest so   2055
And hold him in honor, may heaven reward them—
May the King who commands there care for you all!
If I had leisure to live here a little while longer,
I'd warmly reward you, God willing, myself."
He stepped into his stirrup and swung himself up.   2060
His man passed him his shield, which he slung from
    his shoulder,
And he goads his good Gringolet with shining gilt spurs.

The horse sprang forth on the stones; it stood still no longer
               to prance.
    He met his mounted guide,   2065
    Who bore his spear and lance.
    "May all with Christ abide!"
    He called, and then, *"Bonne chance!"*

The bridge was brought down and the broad castle gates
Unbarred and borne open, swung back on both sides.   2070
He blessed himself briskly and bolted across,
Praising the porter, who knelt to the prince;
"God save you, my lord," the serving man said.
Gawain went on his way, with no one but his guide
To point out the path to that perilous place   2075
And the baneful, hard blow he was bound to receive there.
They ambled by banks where the boughs glistened bare,
Climbing cliffs where the cold clung close to the rocks.
The heavens rose high, but clouds hovered under them;
Mist mantled the moors and melted the mountains.   2080
Each hill wore a hat, a huge hackle of fog.
Brooks boiled and bubbled down hills thereabout,
Breaking their banks and sheeting abroad.
The two wandered their way through the woods as they must,
Till the sun at that season had started to light   2085
              God's vault.
    Then on a hill above a plain,
    Snow-spread, without a fault,
    The fellow with Gawain
    Reined in and bid him halt.   2090

"For I've steered you," he said, "as I should, by my faith,
And now you are nearing that uncanny chapel
That you've searched for so stoutly with such special care.
I must say now for certain in the space I have known you,
I have loved you, my lord, among all living men.   2095
If you act as I urge you, you'll have better luck.
It's perilous, that place that you're pressing to reach.
The one dwelling there . . . there's no worse in the world.

He is sturdy and stern and eager to strike,
Quite the highest and hugest hero on earth.   2100
His body is bigger than the boldest four knights
In King Arthur's house, or Hector, or anyone.[83]
He decrees none may follow their course by his chapel—
Be they never so powerful or prosperous and proud—
But he does them to death with dints of his hand.   2105
He's strong and stern-hearted, a stranger to pity.
Be it chaplain or churl who passes the chapel,
Mild monk or Mass-priest or any man else,
He'd sooner destroy them than save his own life!
So I say, sir, as sure as you sit in that saddle,   2110
Ride there and you're ruined, if he rules the day.
Trust me, it's true, though you had twenty more lives
            to spare,
        For he has lived here long
        Ravening from that lair.   2115
        His buffets are too strong
        For any man to bear.

"So I advise you, my lord, avoid that great varlet.
Pick out another path; do, for God's pity!
Pass on to some place where Christ may preserve you,   2120
And I'll hurry home. You have here my word:
I'll swear by the saints and God's sacraments, too—
'So help me heaven,' and a raft of such oaths—
I'll mislead them mightily and never admit
That you faltered and fled from any foe that I know of."   2125
"Grant mercy,"[84] said Gawain, but then grudgingly added,
"Farewell, good fellow. You wish me good fortune.
I believe you would loyally lie in my cause.
But for all that you say, if I should slink off—
Fight shy for fear and flee as you wish—   2130

---

83. The manuscript gives the name as *Hestor,* which is usually taken to mean Hector of Troy but could also refer to Hector de la Mare, a well-known knight of the Round Table.

84. Short for "God grant you mercy."

I'd be a craven and coward. I couldn't deny it.
I'll go on to the chapel, whatever may happen,
And treat with that tyrant, in what terms I choose,
For doom or delight, as Destiny works
            its will.   2135
      Though he's a gruesome knave
      And though his knocks can kill.
      I know the Lord can save
      His faithful servants still."

"Marry!" said the man, "That's as much as to say   2140
That you'll draw your own doom down on yourself!
If you're so set on dying, I won't seek to stop you.
Have your helm on your head and your hand on your spear,
And ride down this road by the side of that rock,
Till it flattens at length on the floor of the forest.   2145
You'll come to a clearing. In a cove to your left,
You'll see a small slope and sitting above it
The chapel and churlish great champion who keeps it.
Farewell as God wills it, noble Gawain!
All the gold above ground wouldn't get me to go.   2150
I won't fare a foot farther to follow you there."
Then he wrenched round his reins and rode off at once,
Hit his horse with his heels as hard as he could.
Leaping over the land, he left the knight sitting
            alone.   2155
      "By heaven," said Gawain,
      "I'll neither grieve nor groan,
      God's will is surely right.
      So now let it be shown!"

He clucks to his charger and courses ahead,   2160
Clops round a cliff and the copse at its foot,
And rides down rough banks right into the dale.
He looked right and left and lonesome he found it—
No sign of a shelter, search though he might,
But tall cliffs with towering tops on both sides   2165
And rough, jagged rocks, wrinkled ramparts of stone.

The heights overhead seemed to hold up the clouds.
He halted and hitched himself round on his horse
To mark, if he could, a chapel or church.
He saw no such thing, though he thought it was strange,   2170
Save, nearby, a knob or small knoll, as it were—
A smooth, rounded swell by a swift-running brook,
Whose clattering current clanged over the rocks,
Breaking in bubbles like a pot on the boil.
The man urges his horse to the side of the hummock,   2175
Lighting down lightly to loop round the reins
And bind his good horse to a bent linden branch.
He moved toward the mound and meandered around it,
Unsure in himself what the swelling could be.
It had holes at one end and on either side,   2180
With tufts of green turf crowning the top.
The hillock was hollow. It held an old cave,
Or grotto, or gash; he'd give it a name,
                    but can't.
          "Lord in heaven," said the knight,   2185
          "Call this a church? I shan't!
          In there—around midnight—
          The fiend himself might chant!

"My word," Gawain said, "what a woebegone place,
Horrid and ugly—eerie, unkempt!   2190
Fit ground for the knight who goes in green garb
To deal his devotions in devilish wise.
Now I feel in my five wits that it is the fiend,
Who sent this stern test to destroy me today—
A chapel of mischief, may evil chance take it!   2195
The cursedest church I ever came near!"
With his helm on his head and handling his lance,
He roams to the roof of the rough earthen dwelling.
Then from high on the hill, behind a hard rock,
Across the swift current, rose an uncanny noise.   2200
Scritch! The sound screaked as if scoring the cliffs—
As if one on a grindstone were whetting a scythe.

Scritch! It whirred like a weir in high water.
Scritch! It screeched, scathful to hear.
"By God," said Gawain, "these grim goings-on   2205
Are here for my hearing. Yea, made in my honor,
          I say.
     Yet all comes by God's will.
     'Alas,' won't serve today.
     For though my life may spill,
     Fear won't make it stay."   2210

The hero hallooed at the height of his voice,
"Who holds power in this place and will parley with me?
For now good Gawain is awaiting your words.
Anyone who wants aught of me, hasten this way,   2215
Now or else never, to see to his needs."
"Wait!" shouted one on the cliff wall above him,
"You shall have, and in haste, what I offered you once."
Yet he kept on contriving those steel-cutting screeches.
He'd finish his grinding before he came forward.   2220
Then he crossed through a crag, coming down through a crack,
Hurtled out through an opening holding his weapon,
A new Danish axe most apt for their enterprise
With a brutal steel blade that bent round its haft,
Filed to a fine edge and full four feet long—   2225
No less, by the length of the lace down its shaft.
The man and his gear gleamed as green as before—
Legs, face, and loins, whiskers, and locks,
Save he now fared afoot, and firmly he strode,
The head of the axe briskly tapping the earth.   2230
When he came to the water, unwilling to wade,
He vaulted the stream on his axe and advanced,
Fell and fierce, on a field flocked all about
          with snow.
     Gawain beheld the knight   2235
     And bowed, but nothing low.
     His foe said, "As is right,
     You've come to stand your blow.

"Gawain," said the green warrior, "God keep you well!
Surely you're welcome, good sir, to my seat,   2240
And you've timed your travels as true as you should,
Keeping the covenant we cast once between us.
A year ago, truly, you took what I tendered,
And now, at this New Year, I need to repay you.
This valley is empty. We're here on our own.   2245
There's no one to stop us or stay our good sport.
Heave off that helm and have here your payment.
Wield no more words, sir, than I wielded then,
When you hacked off my head with one swipe of your axe."
"By God—" said Gawain, "Who gave me my life—   2250
I'll bear you no grudge for what grim grief befalls me.
If you stop at one stroke, I will stand still,
Nor offer you hindrance, however you work;
                    I swear!"
            He bent his neck and bowed,   2255
            Displayed his nape all bare,
            Like one who went uncowed,
            Too proud to show his care.

Then the grim man in green gathered himself,
And took up his tool to trounce good Gawain.   2260
With all the strength in his sinews he snatched it aloft,
And swung it as stoutly as if to destroy him.
Had he driven as dreadful a dint as he promised,
That doughty good lord would have doubtless lain dead.
But Gawain glanced aside at the glittering blade   2265
As it hurtled to earth to undo his life,
And his stout shoulders shrank away from the steel.
The other broke off and halted his stroke,
Reproving the prince with proud, crowing words:
"You can't be Gawain, so good and so glorious,   2270
Who was never afraid of a foe in the field.
Flinching in fear, before you feel harm!
I don't recall hearing that he could be humbled.
I never blenched, sir, beneath your best blow,
Or called for conditions in King Arthur's house.   2275

My head fell at my feet, but I never flinched,
While you, unhurt, hunker down, quailing at heart.
That makes me, sir, the more manly man,
    well graced."
Gawain said, "I cringed once;   2280
Now I'll stand stoutly braced.
But if *my* head should bounce,
It cannot be replaced!

"But move yourself, man, and do what you must;
Deal me my destiny and do it right quickly.   2285
I'll submit to your stroke and shrink not a whit
Till I'm hewn by that axe—on my honor, I will."
"Have at you then!" The man heaved his axe high,
Mouthing with menace as if he were mad.
He struck a stiff stroke, but stopped the axe short,   2290
Withholding his hand and not harming the knight.
Gawain was left waiting—no wincing this time.
He stood still as stone, or the stump of a tree
Anchored in earth with a hundred twined roots.
The man in green mocked him, merry of mood: 2295
"Ah, your heart's whole again! It behooves me to hack now.
May the high honors help that Arthur awarded you;
Let them save your fair skin, sir, if somehow they can."
Roiling with wrath, Gawain railed at the fellow:
"Bah! Fall to, you felon, you fulminate so   2300
Your heart must be heaving in awe of yourself!"
"In faith," said his foe, "so fiercely you speak,
I'll no longer delay but look to our errand,
    I vow."
He readied his best blow   2305
With frowning lip and brow.
Gawain's heart filled with woe.
No rescue for him now!

The man lifts his blade lightly and launched it down fair,
So the barb of the bit barely brushed Gawain's neck.   2310
The axe hit the ground heavily, but hurt him no more

Than to snick his neck's side and sever the skin.
It flashed through his flesh, cleaving the fat.
Blood spilled on his shoulders and splashed on the ground.
When Gawain saw his shining blood spatter the snow,   2315
He shot from his standing, leaping more than a spear's length,
And heaved up his helm to cover his head.
With a shrug of his shoulders, he shook round his shield
And brandished his blade and boldly called out—
Not since he was born, brought forth by his mother,   2320
Had he been half so happy abroad on the earth:
"Break off!" he barked. "Bluster no more!
I suffered your stroke—stood still, without strife—
If you offer another, I'll amply requite it.
I'll pay you back promptly, I promise you that,   2325
            full bold.
        I owed you just one stroke
        As you yourself, sir, told,
        Before King Arthur's folk,
        So on your honor, Hold!"   2330

The green man gave over and grounded his axe,
Set the haft on the earth, with his hand on the blade.
He looked at the lord standing lightly before him—
How daring, determined, and dauntless he seemed!
Armored and aweless, he pleased the man's heart.   2335
He calls to him cheerfully in a clarion voice.
In ringing, round tones he arraigns the good knight:
"Hold, hero! We'll have no harsh words in this holding.
No one's behaved with dishonor to you;
I have kept the accord that we made at your court.   2340
I was due just one dint, and I drove it—I'm done.
I clear you completely of all other claims.
If I'd cared to, I could have returned you a clip,
A harder, more hurtful one, and done you some harm.
First I offered a flourish, no more than a feint,   2345
But spared your fair skin, and suitably so,
By the pledge that we plighted in play that first night.
Your faith then was faultless; you conferred upon me

All the gains that you got, just as good as your word.
That second feint stood for your scruples next morning: 2350
You consigned me two kisses as well as you could.
For your dealing those days, I dealt two sham blows—
    fair trade.
  True men should pay each debt.
  They needn't feel afraid.   2355
  The third day's why you met
  That touch of this sharp blade.

"It's my garb you've got there, that same woven girdle;
My wife was the giver, as I'm well aware.
I could recount your kisses, your conduct as well—   2360
And all my wife's wooing—I worked it all out!
I sent her to sound you, and you showed yourself
The most faultless fellow who fares on the earth.
As pearls pass white peas in merit and price,
So you stand, sir, yourself, excelling all knights.   2365
Yet you lacked just a little in loyalty there—
Not for the belt's weaving or wooing my wife,
But for love of your life, and little I blame you!"
Stout Sir Gawain stood in study a while,
So smitten by shame he shuddered at heart.   2370
All the blood in his breast rose to blend in his face,
As he shrank, disconcerted by what the lord said.
The first answer he hit on to utter was this:
"Accursed be cowardice and covetousness both!
You are villainy, vice, and virtue destroyed!"   2375
He loosened the girdle of green round his girth,
Flung the belt fiercely, full at his foe:
"Lo, here's my falseness; may foulness befall it!
For care of your carving, cowardice taught me
To give in to greed, forgetting my nature—   2380
The largesse and loyalty belonging to knights.
Now I'm faulty and false, who was always afraid
Of treason and untruth, may both those taste sorrow
    to spare!
  Indeed my acts were base.   2385

My faults have been laid bare.
Restore me to your grace,
And I will take more care."

Then the other lord laughed and lovingly said,
"I hold it made whole, any harm that I had.   2390
You are cleanly confessed, sir, and cleared of your faults.
You paid penance today on the point of my blade.
I dispense with your promise; you're polished as clean
As if you'd not erred since you stepped on this earth.
I give you the girdle and all its gold fringes.   2395
Since it's green like my gown, Sir Gawain, you'll perhaps
Remember our meeting when making your way
Among princes of price, a palpable token
Of the chance of the Green Chapel among chivalrous knights.
Come home to my house now to honor the New Year,   2400
And we'll finish our feast in suitable fashion
                    each night.[85]
    Return, Gawain, please do,
    And make peace with my wife.
    We'll reconcile you two   2405
    And end your secret strife."

"No," said the knight, unknotting his helm
To hoist it off handsomely and thank his good host.
"I've lingered too long here—may luck come your way;
And may God hold you high, in Whose hands lie true honors.   2410
My regards to your graceful and gracious good wife,
Both her and that other, my honorable ladies,
Who so neatly entangled their knight in their nets.
It's no marvel a man can be made to look foolish,
Be wrecked and disgraced by such womanish wiles: 2415
Like Adam on earth when one so beguiled him,
As several did Solomon, and Samson as well—
Delilah dealt him his doom. And David thereafter

---

85. Since the observation of Christmas lasted until Epiphany (January 6), there
were still a few days of feasting left to go.

Was ensnared by Bathsheba and suffered great dole.
Now, if women gulled such men, it would be good   2420
If a lord could love them, yet believe them not.
Those old men were princely. They prospered apace,
More than any under heaven who held a man's life
    since then.
  Yet women fooled them all   2425
  Time and time again.
  If I have had a fall,
  Why, so have better men.

"But your girdle," said Gawain, "God give you thanks,
I will wear for goodwill, not the worth of its gold,   2430
Nor the green sash itself with its silk and its pendants,
Nor for wealth nor for worship nor the weaver's great skill,
But to signal my shame when I see it so often.
When I ride in renown, I'll recall to myself
The fault and the frailty of flesh on this earth—   2435
How its lustings may lead us to lapse into filth.
Thus, when pride puffs me up for prowess of arms,
One look at this love-lace will lower my heart.
But I've one thing to ask you—I hope you don't mind—
Since you're lord of this land where I've lingered so long   2440
(So long and so well—may the All-Wise reward you,
Who holds up the heavens, enthroned upon high),
Please say who you are. I'll ask nothing more."
"I'll tell you, and truly," the tall green man answered:
"Bertilak de Hautdesert, I'm called in my holdings,   2445
Through Morgan la Fay's[86] might, who lives in my manor.
She has come by her craft to great cunning and lore.
Through the magic of Merlin[87] she's marred many men;

---

86. Morgan the Fée, French for fairy. King Arthur's half sister and in many Ar-
thurian stories his implacable enemy with magical powers. Morgan had reason
to hate Guenevere as well. The queen had caused Guiomar, one of Morgan's
lovers, to be exiled. Her ancient appearance here is just one of her guises. She
could make herself look any way she liked.
87. King Arthur's great magician.

For the dearest love-dealings she conducted with him—
That cunning enchanter—yea, your court will have heard   2450
    the same.
    A goddess, high, unbowed,
    'La Fay,' as in her name.
    No high ones go so proud,
    That she can't make them tame.   2455

"She sent me in this semblance to search out your hall,
To plumb your court's pride and prove false or true
The rumors that run of your arrant Round Table.
She sent me—a monster—to shatter your minds,
To cow your Queen Guenevere, kill her with dread   2460
Of that gibbering green man who talked like a ghost
With his head in his hand before the high table.
She's the ancient at home, that old, loathly lady,
But she's also your aunt, King Arthur's half sister—
Born to the Duchess of Tintagel, the one upon whom   2465
King Uther sired Arthur, your excellent king.[88]
So I call on you, sir, come pay court to your aunt.
Rest happy at my house, where every man loves you.
You're fully as welcome, I'm willing to swear,
As any he under heaven, for your honor and truth."   2470
But the knight told him no, and would not be persuaded.
So they clasped and they kissed and commended each other
To the Prince of high Paradise and parted right there
    all cold.
    Gawain on charger keen   2475
    Fares back to Arthur's hold.
    The knight in brightest green
    Went off to parts untold.

---

88. A complicated story. Briefly, King Uther lusted after Igraine, Duchess of
Tintagel, who already had three daughters, including Morgan and Morgause,
Gawain's mother. While at war with her husband, King Uther visited Igraine in
the guise of the duke and fathered Arthur. This left a residue of bad blood be-
tween Arthur and his half sisters.

Wild ways in the world, Gawain must now ride
On Gringolet. He'd been granted his life.   2480
Oft he harbored in houses and often without.
His adventures in vales and the forces he vanquished—
I won't try at this time to tell you their tales.
The hurt soon grew whole that he had in his neck,
Beneath the bright belt he bore draped about it,   2485
Sloping down from his shoulder, secured at his side,
Locked under his left arm, that lace, with a knot,
To signal his shame, the stain of his fault.
Thus he comes to the hall as hale as he left.
What delight the lords felt when they learned he was there!   2490
Good Gawain was among them—they thought that great gain.
The lord kissed his liege, his lady did too,
And many strong knights mustered to meet him.
They ask how he'd fared. He freely confesses
All the cares and encumbrances he had encountered,   2495
What chanced at the chapel, the cheer of the knight,
The love of the lady, and, last, the green lace.
The nick on his neck, he showed to them naked.
He'd earned that dishonor at the lord's strong hands
         with blame.   2500
   He suffered and he blushed;
   He groaned aloud for shame;
   His cheeks grew red and flushed
   When he disclosed the same.

"Behold," said the hero, handling the girdle,   2505
"The blazon of blame that I bear round my neck.
This shows the suffering and shame I've endured
For the coveting and cowardice that cast me so low.
It tells of the untruth in which I was taken.
I must display this green girdle as long as I live: 2510
One may hide a bad act, but hardly undo it.
It fixes so firmly it never falls free."
The king comforts the knight, while his courtly companions
Allay him with laughter and loyally assert

That each lord[89] who belonged to the league of King Arthur,　　2515
Every man of their muster, would have a belt made,
A girdle of green, to gird round his front
For worthy Gawain's sake, to wear in his honor.
That sash was soon seen as the sign of their order:
He was honored who had it forevermore after,　　2520
As written down roundly in the best book of romance.
This tale has been told since King Arthur's time.
The books of Brutus bear it good witness.
Since Brutus the bold was brought here at first
Once the siege and the assault was ceased at Troy,　　2525
　　　　　I say.
　　Many tales since that first morn
　　Have fallen out this way.
　　May He once crowned with thorn
　　Bring us to bliss, I pray! Amen.　　2530

HONY SOYT QUI MAL PENCE[90]

---

89. The manuscript reads *lordes and ladis,* "lords and ladies," but then goes on to equate these persons with the *broþerhede* of Arthur's knights. It seems likely that *lordes and ladis* is simply a mistaken rendering of *lordes and ledes*—"lords and nobles"—by the copyist.

90. "Shame to anyone who thinks evil," the French motto of the Order of the Garter, an honorary society founded by Edward the Third in the mid-fourteenth century. This line was added to the manuscript in a different hand sometime after the original text was finished. It does not really belong to the poem.

Suggestions for Further Reading

Useful General Introductions

Archibald, Elizabeth, and Ad Putter, eds. *The Cambridge Companion to Arthurian Legend.* Cambridge: Cambridge University Press, 2009.

Brewer, Derek, and Jonathan Gibson, eds. *A Companion to the* Gawain-*Poet.* Woodbridge, UK: D. S. Brewer, 1997.

Cooper, Helen. *The English Romance in Time: Transforming Motifs from Geoffrey of Monmouth to the Death of Shakespeare.* Oxford: Oxford University Press, 2004.

Krueger, Roberta L., ed. *The Cambridge Companion to Medieval Romance.* Cambridge: Cambridge University Press, 2000.

Pearl, Cleanness, Patience *and* Sir Gawain. Reproduced in facsimile from the unique manuscript Cotton Nero A.x. in the British Museum. Intro. I. Gollancz. Early English Text Society 162. Oxford: H. Milford, Oxford University Press, 1923.

Putter, Ad. *An Introduction to the* Gawain-*Poet.* London: Longman, 1996.

Scholarship

Aers, David. "'In Arthurus Day': Community, Virtue and Individual Identity in *Sir Gawain and the Green Knight.*" In *Community, Gender and Individual Identity: English Writing 1360–1430,* 153–78. London: Routledge, 1988.

Ashley, Kathleen M. "Trawth and Temporality: The Violation of Contracts and Conventions in *Sir Gawain and the Green Knight.*" *Assays* 4 (1987): 3–24.

Barrett, Robert W., Jr. *Against All England: Regional Identity and Cheshire Writing, 1195–1656.* Notre Dame, IN: University of Notre Dame Press, 2009.

Bennett, Michael J. *Community, Class and Careerism: Cheshire and Lancashire Society in the Age of* Sir Gawain and the Green Knight. Cambridge: Cambridge University Press, 1983.

Burrow, J. A. *A Reading of* Sir Gawain and the Green Knight. London: Routledge and Kegan Paul, 1965.

Crane, Susan. "Knights in Disguise: Identity and Incognito in Fourteenth-Century Chivalry." In *The Stranger in Medieval Society,* ed. F. R. P. Akehurst and Stephanie Cain Van D'Elden, 63–79. Minneapolis: University of Minnesota Press, 1997.

Dinshaw, Carolyn. "A Kiss Is Just a Kiss: Heterosexuality and Its Consolations in *Sir Gawain and the Green Knight.*" *Diacritics: A Review of Contemporary Criticism* 24, nos. 2–3 (1994): 205–26.

Ganim, John. "Disorientation, Style, and Consciousness in *Sir Gawain and the Green Knight.*" *PMLA* 91, no. 3 (1976): 376–84.

Heng, Geraldine. "Feminine Knots and the Other: *Sir Gawain and the Green Knight.*" *PMLA* 106, no. 3 (1991): 500–514.

Heng, Geraldine. "A Woman Wants: The Lady, 'Gawain,' and the Forms of Seduction." *Yale Journal of Criticism* 5, no. 3 (1992): 101–34.

Ingledew, Francis. Sir Gawain and the Green Knight *and the Order of the Garter.* Notre Dame, IN: University of Notre Dame Press, 2006.

Lochrie, Karma. "Tongues Untied: Confession and Its Secrets." In *Covert Operations: The Medieval Uses of Secrecy,* 12–55. Philadelphia: University of Pennsylvania Press, 1999.

Putter, Ad. Sir Gawain and the Green Knight *and French Arthurian Romance.* Oxford: Clarendon Press, 1995.

Trigg, Stephanie. "The Romance of Exchange: *Sir Gawain and the Green Knight.*" *Viator: Medieval and Renaissance Studies* 22 (1991): 251–66.

Weiss, Virginia. "The Medieval Knighting Ceremony in *Sir Gawain and the Green Knight.*" *Chaucer Review* 12 (1977): 183–89.

Editions

Andrew, Malcolm, and Ronald Waldron, eds. *The Poems of the Pearl Manuscript:* Pearl, Cleanness, Patience, Sir Gawain and the Green Knight. 5th ed. Exeter, UK: University of Exeter Press, 2008.

Tolkien, J. R. R., and E. V. Gordon. *Sir Gawain and the Green Knight.* 2nd ed. Edited by Norman Davis. Oxford: Clarendon Press, 1967.